T0209162

Jesus *is* MY HERO

DR. SCOTT RAWLINGS

WESTBOW
PRESS®
A DIVISION OF THOMAS NELSON
& ZONDERVAN

This book is a work of non-fiction. Unless otherwise noted, the author and the publisher
make no explicit guarantees as to the accuracy of the information contained in this book
and in some cases, names of people and places have been altered to protect their privacy.

WestBow Press books may be ordered through booksellers or by contacting:

WestBow Press
A Division of Thomas Nelson & Zondervan
1663 Liberty Drive
Bloomington, IN 47403
www.westbowpress.com
844-714-3454

Because of the dynamic nature of the Internet, any web addresses or links contained in
this book may have changed since publication and may no longer be valid. The views
expressed in this work are solely those of the author and do not necessarily reflect the
views of the publisher, and the publisher hereby disclaims any responsibility for them.

Any people depicted in stock imagery provided by Getty Images are models,
and such images are being used for illustrative purposes only.
Certain stock imagery © Getty Images.

Scripture quotations are from the ESV® Bible (The Holy Bible, English
Standard Version®), Copyright © 2001 by Crossway, a publishing ministry
of Good News Publishers. Used by permission. All rights reserved.

ISBN: 978-1-6642-7019-0 (sc)
ISBN: 978-1-6642-7020-6 (hc)
ISBN: 978-1-6642-7018-3 (e)

Library of Congress Control Number: 2022911588

Print information available on the last page.

WestBow Press rev. date: 08/19/2022

This book is dedicated to:

To my wife, Charlotte! Your love for Jesus is contagious! Thank you for endlessly and graciously supporting everything I do. I love you with all my heart!

To the members of Living Stones Church for having to put up with me for so many years! I love each and every one of you! Your generosity and love for Jesus make me proud to be your pastor and friend!

To the best mother-in-law a son could ever ask for! Thank you, Linda Stewart, for breaking out of your retirement to help edit another paper!

To all those who, for whatever reason, have lost their first true love. I know we all have busy and hectic lives and it is easy to lose sight of the real reason for living. This book is dedicated to those who want to rise above the mundane and do something supernatural in their lives. To believe in a hero again.

CONTENTS

INTRODUCTION

Seeing Jesus
As Our Hero...Again

———⟡———

There is nothing like a good hero story. People love heroes. They love them so much that Hollywood has capitalized on this. Marvel and DC Comics have made billions of dollars making movies based on our favorite heroes. At the writing of this book, Marvel has grossed over 22.5 billion dollars, which amounts to about 980 million per film. DC Comics is a close second. These movies sell because there is nothing like a hero taking on an evil villain that gets our imaginations and emotions flowing. We grew up wanting to be Superman, Wonder Woman, Captain America, or the Black Panther. Those heroes display honor, integrity, strength, and a love for what is right and worthy. Heroes make us see what is wholesome in this world and a desire to right our wrongs and live with the noble and good intentions that our heroes have displayed for us.

I know that not all heroes are alike, nor do we associate with all of them, but there are some that we adore and cannot wait to see on the big screen. Maybe it is because of their wit, or perhaps their cool catch phrases that attracts us to them. Others, we come to love because of their uncanny abilities to see good in this world and want to do all in their powers to help make this place a safer and healthier world.

One thing is sure, as kids we all loved heroes, and we wanted to be like them. On any given Halloween, you can see hundreds of thousands of little children running around in neighborhoods with their candy-obsessed eyes dressed up in superhero costumes. From Iron Man to Super Woman and Thor, they are all out there knocking on doors and looking as cute as buttons. Why? Because little children love their heroes! They crave someone to look up to, to emulate—to worship. Unfortunately, as we get older, hero-worship ends as we run around relentlessly pursuing all the menial tasks that being an adult includes. Life plays no favorites, and all of us are busy with work and kids and, well—stuff. I get it, I really do, but it shouldn't be that way. Hopefully, this book will show us why going back to worshiping our hero is so essential.

This book is for those looking for a hero to follow. It is for those looking for someone who has the power and the ability to not just make our world a better place, but someone who will make us better people. It is for someone looking for a hero who will not only kick down evil's door and bring justice, but someone who will be loving, caring, and kind, even to the less fortunate, or those who think and act differently than we do. We want a hero who will make us his sidekick as we go on adventures together. We want a hero who will bring out the best in us as we dare to do the impossible against supernaturally impossible odds. We want a hero who will show us again how life is meant to be lived. That hero is Jesus Christ!

1

CHAPTER

Something Has to Change

❧

CHURCH IS NOT OUR HERO

I had a problem, and I am talking about a big fat ugly problem. When I became a Christian, I found out early from many other Christians that the church was the be-all and end-all for my Christian faith. Pastors and Christians repeatedly told me that I was supposed to invite people to church. I mean isn't a church where God solely resides and pours out his Holy Spirit on the heathens who need to be there? So from the time I gave my life to Christ at nineteen, I was constantly devoted to bringing people to church. I ended up taking classes at a local church where they taught FAITH, an acronym that means ... well ... umm ... I have no clue; I already forgot it.

Nevertheless, I am sure it was a very clever acronym that stirred my emotions for action. It was an outreach class where we would go house to house every Wednesday evening and invite ourselves into some stranger's home and talk about our church, how wonderful it was, and how they should be there. I am sure there was one single old lady who was influenced by this approach. Still, I don't ever remember seeing the people into whose homes I intruded come to our church.

Later, it was all about "Evangelism Explosion." This approach was meeting random people (mostly at the mall) and forcing them to hear me give a thirty-minute presentation on how they were sinners and how I had all the answers. After the thirty-minute presentation (full of excellent illustrations, I might add), I would encourage them to pray and accept Christ as their Savior. No one ever did. Spoiler alert: it was probably because it took thirty minutes to present.

Not all of that was bad. It taught me how to have the courage to meet anyone and have a conversation about Christ. But I won't lie; it was very discouraging when no one wanted what I was giving. So I went back to the tried and true. Just invite them to church. That was easy and simple.

If we are honest, the church is familiar. The church is home. We know everything about our local church. We know how long the pastor will preach. We know where the children's ministries are. We know where the bathrooms are. Side note: I had a woman working at a previous church's front desk. I am always curious why people go to a particular church when millions are nearby, so I asked her why she ended up here. No joke, she said she loved our church because our *toilet paper* was soft! She said—with a straight face, I might add—that her previous church had rough toilet paper! Who knew?

However, when we make church our hero and not Jesus, we are in for a world of hurt. The church was never meant to be our hero. Jesus is. When we replace Jesus, take the easy way out, and make the church the thing we worship, we become a part of the problem, and it's a big fat ugly problem. For example, I had a neighbor. Let's call him "Neighbor." (Who knows? He might buy this book and read it.) I worked hard to get to know him and invite him to my church. I would tell him what our church was about because the church is familiar, right? As I got to know him better, I kept inviting him to attend our upcoming Christmas Eve service. And guess what? He came! I was so jacked up! I made sure that several of our regulars went up to him and said hello. I wanted him to feel as comfortable as possible, and hopefully, prayerfully, he would enjoy it and come back. In the back of my mind, I imagined he would give his life to Christ and become some super-Christian!

He never came back.

Talk about a total bummer. But worse, I'd built my entire relationship with him around my church, and now that he'd attended once and had never come back—ugh! Talk about awkward. I had no clue what to say to him. I couldn't say, "Hey, Neighbor! What's up? Why did you not come back?" That would make it even more awkward. I did ask him if he liked the Christmas Eve service, and of course, he said he did. I mean, he is not a monster! Did he ever come back? Nope.

After thinking long and hard on this, I have concluded that this person is a complete heathen and will never give his life to Christ! Nah, I am just playing. Maybe.

Think about it for a minute. There are a million possibilities why he never came back. The sermon was too long. The music was too loud. The sermon was boring. The people were overly nice or not nice enough. Maybe traditional music was what he wanted, and contemporary was not his thing. Maybe contemporary was his thing and not traditional. Maybe their kids didn't like the children's ministry. Or the carpet was the wrong color! Who knows why people don't come back to church? I have heard that only one out of ten first-time guests will ever come back to your church. Not sure if that is true, but the odds are that just because you invite someone to church doesn't mean they will ever come back. It is sad, but it is reality.

This taught me a great lesson. What if I'd decided to make Jesus the main talking point with the said neighbor rather than the church I attended? What if I'd told the neighbor about how awesome, caring, and loving Jesus is? What if, when we were talking about how he'd lost his father recently, I'd told him how deeply sorrowful Jesus must feel about his pain and that he was there for him if he ever needed a shoulder to cry on? What if I'd told him that no matter what he was going through, I knew that Jesus was aware and that he cared? If I'd made Jesus the main talking point and not my church, it wouldn't have been awkward when he came to my church once and never returned. It wouldn't have been uncomfortable because our relationship wouldn't have revolved around my church; it would have revolved around Jesus.

Did I do that, though? No! What a blown opportunity!

When we make church our hero and not Jesus, we invest a lot of time and energy in getting our neighbors, coworkers, or family to church. All that work and time for what may be just a courtesy visit and nothing more. They may try it out, but they may never come back. How demoralizing is that? It's probably why most people quit inviting people to come. It is definitely why church attendance is declining all over the United States!

In his book *The Present Future*, Reggie McNeal talks about six tough questions the church must face, and of course, church decline is a major one. McNeal, pointing to several research groups, claims that the churched population has dramatically decreased in each passing decade.[1] The declining trend continues to press on without real solutions to right itself. ARDA, the Association of Religion Data Archives, has taken data on church attendance since 1972, and they would agree with McNeal.[2] Church attendance is slowly dying. Add to the fact that 48 percent of all Americans have no confidence in the church. Is it any wonder that the American culture no longer believes that the church is relevant or any type of real player when it comes to how we live our lives? It's probably why only 26 percent of Americans attend church regularly.[3] And when I say regularly, I mean once a month.

Twenty-six percent!

Once a month!

A columnist for CNBC wrote an article on how the Bureau of Labor Statistics claims that the average American works forty-four hours per week. According to this article, we now work more than any nation in the world.[4] Now, consider that most homes are dual-income; the total hours worked amount to around ninety hours a week. So, not only are people not interested in church, but they are also too busy even to go!

So, what do we do?

Maybe we should go full attack mode and hit every neighborhood close to where we worship with the gospel and start demanding people to come back to church! Alternatively, we can close the doors and spend the next year doing some actual deep discipleship classes where we are equipped with the knowledge of God. Then when we do bust out and encounter the real world, we can have the comprehension and the theological brilliance to answer any question skeptics may ask. I guess we can. I am sure many churches would think that is a great idea. At least it will give them something to do. However, it won't be effective.

Pastors can train people till they are blue in the face. They can give people all kinds of information to load their theological guns. People can receive strategies and methodologies, but none of that will achieve much if we don't love the one who is sending us out.

In the end, it is not about training, it is not about how much we know, and it is not about how well our church is doing attendance-wise. No! It's all about Jesus being our hero. Do we have an all-out devotion and love for him? Is he our first thought when we wake up and the last when falling asleep? Are we craving to get into the Bible to learn more about him? Does our soul become parched when we realize that just an hour on Sunday is not enough to quench the thirst for a hero who has wholly and radically changed our lives? Are we dreaming and scheming of ways in which we can be just like him? If not, then I would suggest Jesus is our Savior, but he is not our hero!

WHY IS JESUS YOUR HERO?

I sat on a god-awful uncomfortable chair at Asbury Theological Seminary in Lexington, Kentucky. I was wrapping up the last year of my doctorate in creating missional communities. To be fair, the chair was probably comfortable; I just had a bad back at the time, so any chair that I was required to sit in for over an hour at a time made me miserable. But I digress. The guest speaker was Mike Frost, an internationally known missiologist and author. He told the thirty or so of us in the room a story that radically changed the way I "do" church.

Mike Frost told us about how he had preached somewhere in Australia, where a young twenty-something came up to him and said, "You make Jesus sound like he is your hero." To which Mike replied, "That is because he is." When the kid asked why, the senior pastor at that church butted in and said, "Can I answer that one?" Mike was happy to oblige since this kid would likely go to this church and wanted this pastor to connect with this young man.

The pastor begins to answer this profoundly essential question as to why Jesus was a hero. And the pastor blew it—big time! He started by saying, "You know, in the beginning...." He begins with Adam and Eve and how sin entered the world. He talked about pain and suffering. Mike noticed how this young man's eyes were beginning to glaze over. He was losing interest. Again, probably one of the most critical questions to ever ask—Why is Jesus your hero?—and this pastor was blowing it. By the time he got to Jesus dying on the cross, the kid was already gone mentally.

Mike Frost then looked at us and with his fiery Australian accent, said,

"People need to know why Jesus is your hero!" He then challenged us. He said, "Can you tell me right now why Jesus is your hero? And you cannot say that he died for your sins!"

Ouch! Now that's not nice to say to a room full of pastors. That is our go-to! Jesus is my hero because he died for my sins! What was worse, it was kind of embarrassing. For a full minute or more, this room of more than thirty pastors from places across the world just sat in silence.

Why is Jesus my hero?

Why is Jesus my hero? We sat in silence, thinking.

After a while, we gathered our thoughts and for the rest of the class shared why Jesus was our hero without mentioning he died for our sins. It was a fun exercise to do and one I would recommend to any church. To hear so many people explain why Jesus is their hero and to realize that so many had reasons that were not my own was powerful. It made me see Jesus in a different light, and it made me understand Scripture in a new way as well.

That night, laying on the little twin-sized bed in the dorm room on campus—well—if you can call it twin-size. Is there a size smaller than a twin? Maybe a crib? I don't know, but it was itty bitty! Laying on the bed, it became clear as day. The reason we are inclined to invite people to church than tell them about Jesus is because we don't understand why he's our hero. For most of that night, I lay there—with my feet hanging off the end—wondering how I could change the culture of our church when for the longest time, I made the church buildings and programs the main thing.

Most churches build a culture around their buildings or programs—or, worse—the lead pastor. What if we decided right here and now to create a culture where Jesus is our hero? What if we create a culture in which we cannot wait to come to church to hear stories about our hero through the preaching of the word? What if we cannot wait to sing to our hero through music? What if we create a culture in which we cannot wait to reconnect with people whose hero is the same as ours? What if we are thrilled to meet in small groups as we share, talk, and do life more deeply with others as we get to know our hero better? What if, in this culture, we make it a habit to come early on Sunday mornings to help set up and serve, on the chance that someone will come to visit who doesn't know Jesus as their hero but will hear about why he is ours? What if, in this culture, we cannot wait to go into our communities and neighborhoods so we can share with our neighbors, our coworkers, or friends why Jesus is our hero? Imagine a culture that brings us delight to feel the presence of God in our lives. A culture where God constantly shows us that others are hurting and broken and need of a hero and that we have what it takes to heal them by telling them about Jesus.

Suppose we cannot answer the question as to why Jesus is our hero (without saying he died for our sins). In that case, we will be hard-pressed to have what it takes to build up a culture in our churches to make any lasting change. Oh sure, you will have several come and visit your church. Your church may even grow a little in attendance, but will it make any lasting impact on your community? Will it make any lasting impact on the members of that church? It is time we stop making the church our hero and begin to worship Jesus as the hero that he is.

That is why for the rest of this book, I want us to see Jesus in Scripture and imagine being his sidekick. Imagine being with him when he walked the hills of Galilee or hiked through the desert mountains to get to Jerusalem. Imagine the thousands upon thousands of people crowded all around him to hear him speak or possibly see a miracle. I want us to lose ourselves to the stories of Christ and be one hundred percent present with Him in his journey as he begins to usher in the Kingdom of God. We will see Jesus not just as a Savior who died for our sins but as a hero who wants us to join him in his heroic mission to change the world.

Something to Think About...

1. Have you ever made your local church community more important than your relationship with Christ? Why do you think some Christians do?
2. Why is it easier to invite someone to church than it is to invite someone to believe in Jesus?
3. Why is Jesus your hero, and you cannot say he died on the cross for your sins?
4. Have you ever shared with someone why Jesus is your hero? If not, why not?

2

CHAPTER

Still A Long Way Off

———— ◆ ————

APPALACHIAN MOUNTAINS

T homas Nelson was my best friend in college. He was the leader
of CRU (previously known as Campus Crusade for Christ) at
Kennesaw State University, where we both attended. Thomas
was a six-foot-four beast of a man who loved to spend most of his time
outdoors. Every winter break during my college years, Thomas and I would
pack about seventy pounds of stuff in huge backpacks, hit the Appalachian
Trail, and camp out for a long weekend as we mapped out and planned the
upcoming semester for CRU. It was fun, exciting, and grueling all at the
same time. The hikes were long, but the scenery and conversations will be
with me forever.

Thomas also had a little brother who was actively involved with the Boy
Scouts and earned his Eagle Scout badge by fifteen. Joshua was like Daniel
Boone and MacGyver, all wrapped in one when it came to being outdoors.
I would trust him with my life if I ever got lost in the woods.

Our college pastor, Alex Kendrick (of the Kendrick brothers who starred
and directed films like *Facing the Giants, Fireproof, Overcomer,* and *War
Room*...yes, that was a shameless name drop), loved to make fun movies for
the college ministry to enjoy. Before Alex moved away to become a star in the

Christian movie world, he constantly made goofy movies and used the College Ministry students as actors. Usually, they were spoofs on current movies that were out in the theaters. The last movie he made as a college minster was a little spoof on the upcoming Indiana Jones movies, and I had the opportunity to star in it. We were heading out to the woods during one of the shoots, and the scene he wanted had us rappelling down a side of a cliff. I had never rappelled before, and even though Thomas knew how to harness me up, I wanted Joshua to do it. Again, I trusted Thomas' little brother with my life.

During my last semester of college, we decided to take a hiking trip deep into the Appalachian Mountains. Joshua wanted to tag along because he was eager to try out his new GPS handheld device. The military had used these devices for years, but it was only recently that they allowed civilians to market and sell them. So, of course, Thomas' little brother wanted one. And they weren't cheap! The basic model costed about $2,500.

We hit the trail and had our camp set up by nightfall. I thought we would light a fire and chit-chat until we called it a night. Nope! Joshua wanted to test out his GPS, and he thought the best way to see how good this little device was, was to use it at night.

"Hey guys, let's bushwhack through the woods about a quarter-mile and then use the GPS to find our way back to camp."

"Bushwhack?"

"Yeah, let's leave the marked trail and walk down the mountain a little bit, and then we can use my GPS to get back here."

"Josh, it's pretty dark; you sure you want to do that?"

"Absolutely. Trust me; this thing won't steer us wrong!"

And I did! I trusted him. I mean, so far, he had never failed me when it came to being outdoors.

Dumb!

We got so lost!

Before we knew it, it was well past midnight, and we'd been wandering lost in the woods for over three hours trying to find our camp. That two thousand dollar piece of junk kept making us go in circles. I cannot tell you how many times Joshua would say, "Okay, it says we are fifty feet from our camp," only to come up more deeply embedded in the forest.

I was two months away from getting married to Charlotte, and I kept thinking I would die of starvation or a bear would take me for a bit of snack.

Worry started to creep in. Would I ever get to experience my honeymoon night with the love of my life? Would my dream of having a daughter and then naming her Charlotte so I could call her "Junior" die with me? I mean, why do only the boys get named after their parents and have the nickname Junior? Why can't my daughter have that? I started to wonder if Charlotte would move on quickly without me and marry some doctor, or will she at least wait until my remains have been found by some hiker a year later? I had no clue, but as we were trudging up another hill, I was exhausted, frustrated, and highly disappointed that Joshua had let me down! Plus, I had to use the bathroom. I was utterly miserable.

By the grace of God, we stumbled into our camp around two in the morning. We would later find out that the GPS worked just fine; it was an operational error. I thought the Boy Scouts were always prepared!

Have you ever been lost before? It is not a fun experience. I don't recommend it to anyone. At first, you think this is exciting, kind of an adventure! However, the fun wears off after a while, and the nerves and anxiety begin to kick in. As we look at Luke 15, we will see three stories of someone or something that was lost and how Jesus responds to it. And it is in these three stories that Jesus' heroic nature shines through.

THE JOY OF HEAVEN

As we look at Jesus being our hero, I want us to start with Luke 15, where Jesus begins a three-part parable on something lost. If you are unfamiliar with this chapter, it begins with Jesus eating a meal with some unlikely people. I say unlikely because here is God in the flesh, eating a meal with some very unsavory people—you know, people who were sinners and common thieves. You would figure that Jesus would surround himself with some lovely church-going people who have it all together and the closest they ever come to saying a dirty word is when they say, "doggone it" when they stub their toe. Not Jesus. He intentionally hangs out with people who don't quite make the "good guy" quota.

In Luke 15:2, the Pharisees and scribes (those were the good church-going people, at least in their minds) were grumbling to themselves, saying, *"This man Jesus receives sinners and eats with them."* They couldn't stand it.

How can Jesus, declaring himself as the Messiah, hang out, spend time, and even eat a meal with the riffraff? Shouldn't he be in Jerusalem schmoozing all the high profile, high ranking religious leaders of his day?

If we view Jesus like most Christians do today, I can see why they were grumbling. For most of us, we think Jesus is too holy, too righteous, and too perfect (which he is!) to hang out with those of us who are not holy, not righteous, and not perfect (but he does!). I don't know if you heard this about Jesus, but he attracted many men and women with dubious reputations. That is a nice way of saying that many people who did not go to church regularly found Jesus captivating. Which is interesting because aren't we supposed to be like Jesus? And yet, in our culture, the church is far from captivating.

Jesus had a draw to him. The religious leaders didn't like this at all. The people drawn to the most influential religious leader of all times were not church folks. They didn't look like church-goers. They didn't talk like church. They didn't smell like church. And their favorite words were probably not church words. Yet, Jesus loved to hang out and eat with them. In the ancient Middle Eastern culture, to eat a meal with someone was to say that you line up with them socially. Eating with them says you are my friends, and I accept you. That is what drove these Pharisees and scribes upset. How dare you eat with the lowlifes! Which, honestly, shows us how utterly out of touch these religious elites were with the heart of God. They were so focused on earthly concerns that they lost their heavenly perspective.

I am not sure what you think about when Christians arrive in Heaven. You might have many thoughts about that. Maybe, you think Heaven will be a place of tranquility. Perhaps we think about peace. Others may say holiness, worship, righteousness, or wonderful fellowship with God, Jesus, and all the believers who came before us. All of that is true. However, Heaven's definitive and inescapable character is summed up in the word joy. Heaven is a place of joy. That means the presence of God is always filled with joy.

When we think about joy, it's all about an outcome of fulfillment. If we think about our own lives, we live and strive for joy. Whatever we do in our lives, whatever we pursue or accomplish, is intended to bring us a certain level of fulfillment and satisfaction. It produces a sense of well-being, delight, or happiness in us when that comes. Ultimately, we feel joy, and we work very hard to create an environment in our lives and with our families where life is enjoyable.

On the other hand, Heaven is a place where each attitude, relationship, and action produce complete and total satisfaction and fulfillment. Therefore, it will always have perfect joy. That's why Romans 14:17 says, *"The kingdom of God is…righteousness, peace and joy."* Joy! Heaven is a place of all-embracing joy.

One of the most incredible elements and one of the most significant parts of joy in Heaven comes when people come to know Jesus as Lord and Savior. When those who are lost are found. That is why Luke 15 is a crucial chapter in the Bible—and by far my absolute favorite! To address the religious elite's grumblings, Jesus gives three parables. Three stories as to why he has chosen to eat with these people. Three stories about why he wants to hang out with people like these. There will be something lost, something found, and a party being thrown in each story.

Now, to understand why Jesus is our hero, we need to realize that these three stories are Jesus explaining why he befriends the people that he does. He explains why these people are valuable to him and why he has joy in pursuing these people. We will see that Jesus places a high premium on people who tend to wander and get lost, who believe that they are not good enough. This high premium comes solely because it brings Jesus joy to seek and save the lost.

PRONE TO WANDER

> So he told them this parable: "What man of you, having a hundred sheep, if he has lost one of them, does not leave the ninety-nine in the open country, and go after the one that is lost, until he finds it? And when he has found it, he lays it on his shoulders, rejoicing. And when he comes home, he calls together his friends and his neighbors, saying to them, 'Rejoice with me, for I have found my sheep that was lost.' Just so, I tell you, there will be more joy in Heaven over one sinner who repents than over ninety-nine righteous persons who need no repentance (Luke 15:3-7).

This is a simple parable to understand. You have a hundred sheep, one of them wanders off. The shepherd goes and finds it and then brings it back and throws a party for the lost sheep that is now back in the fold. Pretty simple. The lost has been found.

The Bible talks a lot about being lost. For the most part, I would assume that Christians probably think that if someone is lost, it must mean that they either wanted to get lost or they did something terrible. We have this weird view of seeing lost people as either bad people or angry atheists who scoff in the face of God. However, if we are truly honest with ourselves, I think it is so easy to get lost for the sole reason that you and I are prone to wander. GASP! I know, right? The audacity to say that Christians are prone to wander and get lost!

Nevertheless, it is true. How often have we found ourselves wandering, only to realize I have not been in church in a while? Of course, we will justify it and say, well, my kids! Those whippersnappers! They have all these club sports, and some of their games are on Sunday. It is not like I am wandering from God; I am just trying to love and support my family. I will be back to church soon, I promise. Be honest with yourself. How often do we see ourselves slowly moving away from Jesus as we pursue other things happening in our lives? Yeah, we do it all the time!

It is easy to get lost.

We are all prone to wander.

Wandering is in our nature. This is probably why the Bible mentions sheep over 500 times. For the most part, sheep are seen as a metaphor for our human nature. Unfortunately, sheep are not the brightest bulbs on the planet. Sheep are easily distracted and vulnerable animals. Sure, they do their best, but it's in their nature to wander off, which is probably why the Bible likens God to a shepherd over a hundred times in the Bible. God knows that you and I, and even those dreadful "lost" people in our neighborhoods, are prone to wander.

One of my all-time favorite hymns is "Come Thou Fount of Every Blessing." I don't know why I am drawn to this song, and to be honest, I am not much of a hymns guy, but this song gets me every time. Maybe it's because I have been prone to wander all my life, even after becoming a Christian. This song was written by Robert Robinson in 1758 when he was twenty-two years of age. The whole premise of this song focuses on God's divine grace to those who are lost and in need. He was inspired by the verse in 1 Samuel 7:12 that states, "*Then Samuel took a stone and set it up* between *Mizpah and Shen and called its name Ebenezer; for he said, 'Till now the LORD has helped us.'"* Ebenezer is a Hebrew word that means stone of help. But what gets me every time is the fourth stanza.

> *O to Grace how great a debtor*
> *Daily I'm constrained to be!*
> *Let Thy goodness, like a fetter,*
> *Bind my wandering heart to Thee.*
> *Prone to wander, Lord, I feel it,*
> *Prone to leave the God I love;*
> *Here's my heart, O take and seal it,*
> *Seal it for Thy courts above.*

If we think about those words and dwell on them, I am confident we all have felt that way. We all have wandering hearts that are not just prone to wander, but they are prone to leave the God we love. How often, without even noticing, have we wandered from God? It will be too many times to count if you are like me. We all are prone to wander.

In Psalms 23, King David, a shepherd once himself, begins this psalm by saying, *"The LORD is my shepherd; I shall not want"* (Psalms 23:1). This opening line in the psalm is the main reason why you and I have wandering hearts. Do you want to know why people are not captivated by church anymore? Or why people couldn't care less about Jesus? Or why do people get lost? Or why you and I are prone to wander and leave the God we love? It is because we WANT! You and I, we wander because we want. We wander because we think we need more, desire more, or believe there must be more. That is the nature of a sheep.

A sheep will spend on average seven hours grazing, and they can eat about 2.5% - 3% of their body weight per day.[1] Take in the fact that sheep in the Middle East are trying to graze in an arid and desert climate where they are hard-pressed to find enough to sustain them. Thus, they wander. The sheep wake up, graze, move to another place, and graze more. It is a constant moving and eating, moving, and eating. I eat here, but I want more, so I will move over here and eat some more. All-day. Every day. They are never satisfied. The reality is that sheep will constantly wander because they haven't found contentment. They haven't found satisfaction.

Their bellies are not full, so they want more. It is the same reason why we wander. We lack contentment with what we have, and so we crave more. We wander because maybe we think we don't fit in, so we move to another place to graze. We wander off because we don't feel valuable. We wander off because we don't feel loved. We wander off because we don't think our church community meets our needs.

That is why King David, over a thousand years ago, said:

> *Even though I walk through the valley of the shadow of death,*
> *I will fear no evil, for you are with me; your rod and your staff,*
> *they comfort me. You prepare a table before me in the presence*
> *of my enemies; you anoint my head with oil; my cup overflows.*
> *Surely goodness and mercy shall follow me all the days of my*
> *life, and I shall dwell in the house of the Lord forever* (Psalms 23:4-6).

David says that even though we may feel like we are not valued and have this itch to wander, we can stand firm knowing we have a God who will allow the grazing to end! He is our Ebenezer, our Stone of Help, who will be with us in the hills and valleys, the good times and the bad. He is God who looks out for our best and will extravagantly provide for us with only the best! Where his mercy and goodness will follow us all the days of our lives. In other words, we don't have to want anymore. We don't have to wander off anymore. Jesus will provide us with satisfaction, fulfillment, and joy to the point where our wandering eyes no longer crave grazing elsewhere. *The Lord is my shepherd, I shall not want* (Psalms 23:1).

Psalms 23 shows how much our God values us. If we ever think we have no value in the eyes of God, then we have lost our minds. We mean the world to him! We are everything to him! There is not a place on this earth that we can wander off to where He won't find us, pick us back up, and take us back to where our souls will find satisfaction and joy again. Psalms 23 is the character of God being put on display for sheep like you and me. It's the main reason why Jesus won't hesitate to leave the 99 to come and find the one prone to wander. That is why when the Pharisees were grumbling because of the company Jesus was keeping, he wasn't afraid to let them know that just because they didn't approve of them doesn't mean he will.

What is sad is that the church in our culture does a lousy job of seeking out sheep prone to wander. We are even worse when seeking the Christian sheep who tend to wander off. I know, I know—if you are a pastor reading this, you are going, "NOT TRUE!" We offer up fantastic programs at our church for the sheep to come. We have a rockin' Student Ministry and a kickin' Children's Ministry for those sheep to drop their kids off while we wow them with our smoke machines, loud music, and hip-looking lead pastor! I mean our pastor even has tattoos to relate to the millennial sheep in our church! We even have a coffee shop where people can come and sip some brew and chat with one of our five million staff members. It is not our fault that sheep don't want to come to us! We work hard at getting those sheep to come to us!

Furthermore, when they don't—well—maybe it is because they are one of those "bad" sheep. And—well—don't tell anyone this, but we probably don't want them anyway. They might mess up things around here or steal our life-size olive wood church nativity we got back in 1999 from Bethlehem that we now have rested on a large pedestal in the center of our Corinthian marble foyer.

I jest.

Sort of.

Jesus, on the other hand, is looking at these religious leaders going; I never asked you to create fancy programs to draw in the sheep. Never once did I say that. Instead, he is encouraging us to leave our church buildings and fancy programs and go and find the sheep and hang out with them. Eat with them. Why? Because everyone is prone to wander.

Luke 15:5 says, "*And when he found it* [the sheep], *he lays it on his shoulders, rejoicing.*" I love that verse. Not **IF** he finds the lost sheep, **WHEN**! Why? Because a good shepherd has no alternative. Most shepherds back then were hired to watch a flock, but they were not the flock's owners. In the book of Exodus, if a shepherd was careless and lost a sheep, he had to pay that owner back the price of that sheep. Shepherds, knowing their responsibility, are not lazy or indifferent to the sheep. Nor are they unafraid to go looking for the one that wanders. Good shepherds understand the wilderness the sheep get lost in because they spend their days and nights out there. They know the dangers of wild animals that prowl around at night, and yet they don't think twice about going and seeking that sheep until it is found, no matter how strenuous or complicated the task. Each sheep is precious in the shepherd's eyes. Leaving the 99 and going after the one was not optional for shepherds. Nor is it optional for Jesus. That's why he is my hero!

JESUS IS MY HERO BECAUSE HE WILL RELENTLESSLY PURSUE ME EVEN WHEN I TEND TO WANDER OFF

What kind of God is so patient and tolerant to demonstrate his love for us that he would drop everything and come after us when we wander? What kind of God sees all people as supremely valuable? And then we have to ask, why? Why does he do it? Why would Jesus come after me when I am just a nobody? I mean, as a Christian, I should know better than to wander off, so it makes more sense to me if Jesus is mad at me or angry at my lack of Christian discipline. But he doesn't get mad. He sees me as his child, his beloved, his love, and every time I wander off, he comes and gets me. He knows my wandering heart and yet his love for me is preposterous, as he continues time and time again to run after me when I wander and direct me back to him.

Why? Because it is what brings him joy. *"Just so, I tell you, there will be more joy in heaven over one sinner who repents than over ninety-nine righteous persons who need no repentance"* (Luke 15:7). On behalf of God, there is no greater joy than going after the sheep who are prone to wander. Even Christian sheep who are prone to wander.

Those religious people who were grumbling and saying that Jesus was eating with the sheep. Of course Jesus would eat with them, he is not like the Pharisees and scribes who were so indifferent and disinterested in the sheep. They didn't even care if they were ever recovered or not. For the most part, they didn't even care if they kept wandering off as they grazed, as long as they didn't show up to their well-manicured programs! But I tell you, it brings Jesus joy to be with them! It is Heavenly bliss to go after those who wander and bring them back into his loving arms. So yes! Jesus does eat with them! And he will continue to eat with them! They are his, and he will never let them go!

Every time I read Luke 15, I am always blown away by this story. If that was all the Bible had to say about Jesus, he would be my hero for life. Praise God for our Good Shepherd, who is not afraid to get his hands dirty coming after me when I wander. How I love him for that! How I need him when I do! Praise God that we have a hero who will constantly and relentlessly come looking for us! We need to be reminded that Jesus will never let us out of his sight. We need to be continually reminded that it is never too far for him, no matter how far away we may have wandered off. That is why he is my hero because God knows I have wandered off, and I know it is in my nature to do so again.

Something to Think About...

1. In Luke 15:1-2, what is the response of the Pharisees when they see all of the tax collectors and sinners drawing near to Jesus? Why do you think they responded in this way? Do you think some churches are like these Pharisees when it comes to reaching out to those who are lost?
2. How are we like the sheep who have wandered off? How are we like the shepherd who leaves the comfort of the flock to go looking for the lost sheep?
3. Did the sheep do anything in this story in Luke 15? What does this tell us about salvation? How does this affect how we see ourselves and the lost people in our community?
4. Is it possible to assume that our church culture is declining because we have lost the joy of the Lord in seeking the lost?
5. Is there someone you know that needs rescuing? What steps will you take to go and lead that person to the Good Shepherd?

3

CHAPTER

You're So Irrational

━━━◆◆◆━━━

I LOST MY SON

Have you ever lost something? I cannot count how many times I lost something. I have lost my car keys and phone on numerous occasions. Praise God the Apple Watch, once synced with your phone, has a button that will ping your phone when you lose it. My wife uses that button about five times a day. Sometimes the phone is next to her, and she will ping it. Honestly, it has saved me countless hours of getting up and helping my wife find her "lost" phone.

I can't tell you how many times I lost the remote control to the TV or socks to the nefarious dryer. But those are little things that we can get over quickly if we lose them. However, we lose other things that are much harder to move on and forget. For example, I lost my dignity when I was in the 10th grade. I was in a drama class, and my older brother Kevin decided to take the class with me, despite being a senior. I am sure he took it just to bother me and make me look dumb in front of my classmates.

During the midterms, we were given a drama presentation of our choosing. Kevin and I decided to team up and do it together since we lived together and could work on it at home. The course was pretty easy, and our drama teacher was very lenient and would allow us to get away with a lot of stuff, as long as we didn't kill anyone. Probably one of my favorite classes I took in high school before my brother stripped me of my dignity.

My brother thought it would be funny to de-pants me in front of everyone during the presentation. Kevin and I agreed that I would go first, so while I was "acting" away, Kevin moved behind me, grabbed a handful of my shorts, and yanked down hard! Now, I am a boxer and not a briefs guy. I have no scientific reason why I like boxers over briefs, but I do. I know several people who prefer briefs, and you will get no judgment from me. You do you! So, when Kevin pulled my shorts down, I knew I was wearing my good boxers (you know, the ones that were clean and didn't have any holes in them), so I decided to play it cool and just kept on giving my presentation as if nothing happened, despite the whole class cracking up laughing.

I was a true professional actor.

What caught me off guard, though, was the horror on the face of our drama teacher. I saw her take a deep breath as if she was about to scream something. She was in the process of standing up when I decided to look down and see what Kevin did to me. Sure enough, Kevin de-pants me all right, but not only did he pull my shorts down, but he also managed to pull my boxers down with it. I also happened to be wearing a shirt that was a little short for me, but I liked that shirt!

Yeah, I lost my dignity that day.

Losing my dignity in drama class was not my only loss.

I also lost my girlfriend. She was a beauty, too! We've been dating for about a month, and I was driving her home one night after a lovely night at a fancy restaurant (Taco Bell). For my 17th birthday, my dad bought me a used 1971 fire engine red VW bug. It essentially broke down every other week. It was a piece of junk that probably topped out at about 50 miles an hour if I was going downhill! No joke, after I became a Christian, I went to buy anointing oil at the local Christian store to pour it all over the engine. I needed some divine help because apparently, my car loved to break down, specifically when I was on a first date with a girl. Did I mention that I also lost all confidence as a teenager?

Sure enough, my car broke down, taking this girl home. We were about a mile and a half from her house, and she decided it would be "cute" to walk home. I left my car on the side of the road, hoping someone would steal it so my dad would get me a new one. As we turned the corner on her street, I noticed a car parked in her driveway that I knew didn't belong there. As we got closer, I also saw that someone was leaning up against the said car. As we neared the driveway, I noticed it was her ex-boyfriend leaning up against his perfectly working automobile.

This cannot be good!

A million things went through my head. First off, this kid was much bigger and stronger than me. Second, I was sure he wanted to beat the living daylights out of me for taking away his girl. Third, I might be able to beat him in a footrace if it came to that. My girlfriend noticed him too and intentionally decided to wrap her arm around mine as if claiming me before this intruder.

As we approached her house, he casually sprung from the car he was leaning on and started to walk towards us. I didn't know what to do, so I said the first thing that popped into my head.

"Hey, is that your car?"

"Yeah," he said as he kept walking toward me.

"Umm…do you think you can give me a ride home?"

"What?"

Thankfully that threw him for a loop, and he stopped walking.

"Yeah, my car broke down, and I need a ride home. I'm about five minutes away. Can you give me a lift?"

"Are you serious?"

"Unfortunately, I am very serious."

God does work in mysterious ways. The guy took me home in his perfectly working car. We said maybe two words the whole way to my house, which consisted of "Thanks" and "Yep." Furthermore, considering how my girlfriend promptly broke up with me the next day, I assume Mr. I Got A Working Car, went back to her house, and smoothed things over with her. Yeah, I lost my girlfriend because my car hated me!

I also lost my son at SeaWorld. I am sure I didn't win the dad-of-the-year title that year. Charlotte and I decided to take our kids to SeaWorld to see all the animals and enjoy a lovely weekend away. It was a hot day, I was getting hungry, and Charlotte took her sweet time holding my daughter while showing her every dolphin she could find at the dolphin exhibit. Our son was by her side, so I went to look for a little shade to get out of the heat.

A couple of minutes later, Charlotte was strolling our daughter toward me, and I noticed that our son was not with her.

"Where is Ethan?"

"I thought he was with you."

"I just came here to grab some shade. He was with you when I left. Where is he?"

The look in Charlotte's eyes told me everything I needed to know. It showed absolute fear and a whole lot of anger. Her eyes were communicating to me that if I did not find *her* son, she would personally see to my untimely demise. I instantly leapt to my feet and sprinted back to the dolphin exhibit. Our trip was during the summer, and it was crammed full of people walking and talking everywhere. Frantically, I started looking and yelling out my son's name.

I am still not sure how long this went on, but it felt like forever. My firstborn was missing. Every imaginable scenario went through my head. He was kidnapped. He fell into the water and got eaten by dolphins. He must be terrified that he lost his parents, and he was hiding and crying somewhere, to the point he would need therapy for the next ten years. I felt like I was going to throw up. I heard Charlotte yell, "Ethan!" And the way she yelled it, I could tell by the intonation of her voice that it wasn't a fearful yell but more of an excited shriek. As if she found him and was running in for an embrace!

"Ethan!" Charlotte screamed.

"Yes?"

It sounded as if he was right next to me. I looked all around, wandering why Charlotte was yelling his name but looking at me. Then I felt the gentlest of tugs on my shorts. I looked down, and there was Ethan, standing right next to me as if he had no cares in the world.

"Where were you!"

"I was right here."

"No, you weren't!"

"Yes, I was."

"Fine! But you thought it was okay not to say anything when you heard me yelling your name!"

"I thought you wanted to show me another dolphin, but I've already seen them all."

Kids!

As we look at the following parable in Luke 15, Jesus is going to show us a woman who lost something. She lost something that had significant value to her, and as a result, we will see Jesus' heroic nature shine through.

IRRATIONAL LOVE

"Or what woman, having ten silver coins, if she loses one coin, does not light a lamp and sweep the house and seek diligently until she finds it? And when she has found it, she calls together her friends and neighbors, saying, 'Rejoice with me, for I have found the coin that I had lost.' Just so, I tell you, there is joy before the angels of God over one sinner who repents." (Luke 15:8-10)

The second parable Jesus gives to explain the joy he has when the lost are found is a parable of a woman who lost a coin. Another simple story. A woman lost a coin and looked frantically for it. She finds it and then throws a party because she found it. However, these three short verses tell us that Jesus has an irrational love for people—all people!

Ask yourself this question: How valuable are you? How valuable are we as individual humans? Or ask, how valuable are some of the people you know? Maybe your friends or your co-workers. And then I want you to ask yourself, based on Jesus' viewpoint, what is the value he places on you? What is the value he places on your neighbor's life? How about the value Jesus places on people who go to church? Or those who don't go to church?

For the most part, we have a very irrational approach to value.

When I think about all the material things I have in life, I have difficulty placing value on them. Of course, my wife and children are precious to me. Additionally, my car is valuable and having functioning air conditioning in my house in the sweltering Texan heat during the summer when it reaches over 100 degrees is very valuable. Those are not irrational things. However, when it comes to the regular stuff around our house, I have difficulty placing value on them.

For me, I am what you call a thrower. I throw things away, give them away, or donate them to someone or some organization. My wife, on the other hand, is not a thrower. We don't usually fight, but when we do it starts with, "Hey Scott, where are my…?" For example, not too long ago, my wife approached me and said, "Hey Scott, where are my suits?"

"Your what?"

"My dress suits. Where are they?"

Now a little background here. When Charlotte and I first got married—over 22 years ago—she worked in the professional world where she had to wear slacks and jackets and all that. Back then, jackets had these big fluffy shoulder pads in them. When she wore them, she looked like every placekicker on a football team: skinny with broad shoulders. Praise Jesus; shoulder pads went out of style! Anyway, Charlotte bought herself several professional outfits.

Over twenty-two years ago!

Since then, she has left that field, spent close to ten years as a stay-at-home mom, and now she is a teacher who doesn't have to wear any of those outfits. So, a while ago, I cleaned things up and took some clothes to Goodwill. Those suits may or may not have been with those clothes. I will neither confirm nor deny it. But they are missing. And for some reason, my wife wants them. I have no clue why she wants them, but she wants them, and she wants them now!

"Scott, where are my suits?"

I am a thrower!

I got in trouble one time because my wife spent a lot of time, energy, and creative prowess writing a beautiful birthday card for my birthday. It was well written and filled with an emotional and lovely sweetness. I read it and loved it. Then I threw it away. Don't judge me! I will not be that guy who has a drawer full of birthday cards that I will never look at or read again. That's absurd, and who does that? A couple of days later, my wife found that birthday card in the trash and unloaded on me! HOW DARE YOU!

I now have a drawer filled with birthday cards.

I also have boxes of clothes in my attic that my oldest son outgrew. My wife is adamant that our youngest son will wear them one day, even though they are six years apart. This means they will be in our attic for the next six years, just waiting. Yeah, you don't have to say it. I know! In six years, we will have forgotten all about those boxes because they are now covered with other boxes of "valuable" stuff, and we will end up buying my youngest son new clothes.

Whatever!

How many of us place value on something that honestly you couldn't even give away if you wanted to? Something that, for some reason, has value to you even though it is irrational. Maybe it is a pair of blue jeans that don't fit, but one day! They're my favorite! Perhaps it is a knick-knack you got when you were a kid. Or an old stuffed animal. We have an old Raggedy Ann doll, about four feet tall that one of my wife's relatives made for her when she was younger. Since it was handmade, it resembles a Raggedy Ann doll, but a few things are just not right about it, which makes it look creepy and scares the bejesus out of my kids! For some reason, though, my wife has placed a high value on that doll, and we cannot get rid of it. It has now found a nice, secluded place in the garage where it can scare all the spiders that make their home in the corners of our walls.

I think many of us have an irrational view of what we value. This woman in the parable is no exception. She has a very irrational approach to value. She has ten coins, and she loses one of them. If you were at her house and saw her tearing up the place for one missing coin—ONE COIN—you might think she had lost her mind, or this one lost coin must have been some rare coin worth millions. I would get her frantic state if she had a coin collection and lost half of them, but this is just one coin like all the other coins.

But it gets worse.

She was looking for this coin the way I looked for my lost son at SeaWorld, frantically going mad. Most scholars will say that her coin was just worth a day's wage.[1] How long did she search for this coin? Maybe the whole day. I mean, she could have earned another coin by the time it took her to find the lost one. If you step back for a minute, you have to say that her affection and determination for this coin are not consistent with the actual—literal—value.

She ends up finding it, but then it gets insane. Notice what she does in Luke 15:9, *"And when she has found it, she calls together her friends and neighbors, saying, 'Rejoice with me, for I have found the coin that I had lost.'"* The irrational value she placed on that coin made her throw a party with all her friends and neighbors, which most likely cost more than the coin's actual value. That doesn't make any sense.

Now, why is this story relevant in relation to Jesus hanging out with the people he hangs out with? The message of this parable is that Jesus places value on people so overwhelmingly unlike us. Jesus sees things as valuable where we see them for the most part as something we would just shrug off and move on. Whatever. Who cares? We so easily dismiss things or people as valuable; Jesus doesn't! We look at this woman, and we are like, "Hey, you still got nine coins, and nine out of ten is not bad. So, you lost one; who cares. Move on. Don't destroy your house over this. It is not a big deal."

Not Jesus. Jesus is showing us that he will take apart a whole house to find that which is missing.

JESUS IS MY HERO BECAUSE HIS LOVE FOR ME IS IRRATIONAL

Jesus is very loving and caring, full of mercy and grace, but when you think about it, Jesus can be very irrational.

This coin that this woman lost had value to it. But the value of the coin was just a day's wage. She was acting like that coin was immeasurable. However, it makes sense to think about the irrational value you place on things. Everything that we own, everything that is of worth to us, will have a value that we have determined. My wife put a high value on her dress suits, my eldest son's clothes, and her creepy Raggedy Ann doll. She decided the value of those. I sure didn't! But her value was not determined by how much she could get for it but by how much she said it was worth. For her, it was worth more than the actual value of those items, which didn't matter because they meant something to her. What Jesus is telling us here with just a couple of verses is that the people he is eating with—the tax collectors and sinners—and us as well, have a value to him that is infinite.

Think about that!

Your value in the eyes of Jesus is immeasurable. Your neighbors are incalculable. Your co-workers, friends, and family—infinite. This means we have infinite value in the eyes of Jesus Christ. Stop! Don't keep reading!

Pause and think about that. Your value in the eyes of Jesus is immeasurable. How amazing is that!

Do you want to know what is even odder about this story? Though this plain-Jane, ordinary coin was not easily found, the pursuit of finding it was relentless. Luke 15:8 says, *"Or what woman, having ten silver coins, if she loses one coin, does not light a lamp and sweep the house and seek diligently until she finds it?"* The image here is that this woman was in a panic. She rushed around and lighted the wick of a little clay lamp, going around frantically looking for this coin. She got her little twig broom and started sweeping like a madwoman on the hard dirt floor. She looked in every nook and cranny and every corner of her house. Maybe it fell in a crack? Perhaps it's hiding in the dirt, or it got kicked under a rug? Could it be behind the bed or dresser? She searched diligently. In Greek, it is the word *epimelos*. It means having a critical and urgent sense of care. She moved everything, lifted everything, and searched everything, desperately trying to find this missing coin.

Did she keep searching till she got tired and gave up? Maybe she got hot, sweaty, and uncomfortable, so she called it a day? No! She kept going until she found it! I cannot tell you how many times I have met people who believe that Jesus gives up on them. Jesus doesn't know how to give up! He never gets fatigued or weary, searching diligently for those of us who are prone to wander or get lost. He never gives up! His love for us is irrational!

His approach is so much different from ours. Think about what happens when we lose something? If it is not our car keys or our phone, we usually think, oh well! I know it will show up somewhere. And if not, I guess I need to buy a new one. That's our nature. But Jesus? Because of our value to him, his attitude toward us is relentless. It's irrational. It is illogical. It is this irrational love that attracted me to him. I didn't become a follower of Jesus until I was nineteen, and to be honest, I was not looking for him. Yet, it was the overwhelming value he placed on me that captivated me. And before I knew it, he swept me into his arms, proclaiming that I was his! You were lost, Scott, but now you are found! Come, let's party!

The undeniable truth of this parable is that Jesus is outrageously in love with us simply because the love and value he places on us are immeasurable, infinite, and completely irrational. That is why he is my hero!

Something to Think About...

1. In the parable of the coin in Luke 15, Jesus showed us that the woman placed irrational value on a coin to demonstrate his immeasurable love for us. Why do you think Jesus' love for you is irrational?
2. We see how this coin was not easily found, but the search was relentless. How often do we forget that Jesus relentlessly pursues us? Why is that?
3. Do you know someone that has been misplaced like that coin? What steps will you take to go and relentlessly search for them? What will you do when you find them?
4. Why do you think it is easier to ignore or let go of people different from you? What can we do to see those people as Jesus does?

4

CHAPTER

A Long Way Off

———◆———

DON'T

There is a cute little book Charlotte and I read to our children called "Pooh's Little Fitness Book" by A. A Milne and Ernest H. Shepard. To see plump little animals try to do exercises was amusing to me and the kids enjoyed it. But there is one part of the book that stuck with me. It provided a truth I have tried to live by for most of my life. It spoke to my soul as if the Holy Spirit Himself whispered in my ear. On one page was Eeyore the donkey. Above his sullen head was a caption that said "Eeyore's Exercise Tip for Running." And below was a quote from Eeyore that said, "DON'T!" I love that! Don't run. Running is dumb and makes your sides hurt. Not worth it! Honestly, I hate running. Running should be meant for people who find themselves in a dark alley doing something they know they shouldn't be doing, and some wicked vampire comes chasing them. That should be the only time you should be running.

As a pastor, I try to connect to the members of our church, and I happen to live in the suburbs of Katy, Texas, where everyone looks like Barbie and Ken. Everyone is healthy, fit, and good-looking. Thankfully, I was very skinny growing up and didn't have to work hard to look fit. It was all a sham, but no one knew. That was until I started to get a little bit of a pudge in my belly. I won't lie; at first, I was kind of excited about it. For years, I was nothing more than a bean pole. I think I was 135 dripping wet when I got married. So yeah, I was excited to see a little belly. Over the years, though, that belly started to expand more and more to the point where some members of our church came and asked if I would like to run in a half marathon with them.

"Scott, we are getting a group to run the half marathon in San Antonio in January. You want to come with us?"

"You mean to cheer you on?"

"No, dummy! To run it with us."

"You want me to run a half marathon?"

"Yeah!" *As he looks at my belly!!*

"NO!"

"Why not?"

"Because Eeyore said so."

"What?"

"Never mind. Yeah, fine. I'll do it. But I won't be happy about it."

It was the dumbest thing I had ever done. They asked me during the summer when the heat was about three degrees below the sun's surface temperature. They showed me this app with a coach for a 5k plan to move to a 10K run. The first week was great. Run a minute and then walk for two minutes. I could do that all day! But then it progressed to longer and longer runs. Eventually, the temperature outside was too much for my hairy body to handle, so I decided to run at our neighborhood gym. They had about two dumbbells and two treadmills. So I used the treadmill while I enjoyed the nice air-conditioned room.

I remember one day, about two months before the half marathon; I was jogging on the treadmill doing a seven-mile run. Seven miles straight! Who knew I could do that! After about five miles, I decided to pick up the pace. I am an excellent ten-minute mile guy. I never thought I had to impress anyone to run faster than that. Not too fast, but not too slow. But this day, I thought I could run faster. I was feeling good. So I bumped up the 6.0 on the treadmill to 7.5. I ran that mile and still felt good, so I decided to go wild, and I bumped it up to 9.5 for my last mile. That would put it at a little over a 6-minute mile. I was moving and running faster than I ever had. It was going great for about 30 seconds until the treadmill decided to malfunction and come to a complete stop. Not like a gradual stop, but an abrupt and total halt. I slammed into the front of the machine, which made me bounce backward and fall to the floor. It totally caught me off guard.

I picked myself off, got on the other treadmill, and finished my last mile. I felt good and was thankful no one was in there with me when I bit it. I got home, showered, and then went to work. I slept like a baby that night, only to get back up and hit the treadmill again. I was going to kill this half marathon. I got on the treadmill, cranked it back to 6.0, and jogged. Only now, I began to feel pain in my foot.

Something was not right.

It started to hurt so bad that I had to quit. I decided to take a week off and try again. After a week, it was still hurting. I then took two weeks off, and it was still not healed. After the doctor told me to wear a boot for two weeks, I finally ran again, but by then, the half marathon was less than a month away. There was no way I was going to run straight for 13.2 miles. I eventually decided to run for seven minutes and walk for three minutes throughout the whole race. All my Barbie and Ken church members smoked me. Even my wife, who didn't have the time to train as I did, decided she would speed walk with a friend through all of it, and wouldn't you know it, they almost beat me. I think in the end, they were about two minutes behind me.

So embarrassing.

For the record, this was the last time I ran a half marathon.

Also, the last time I ran on a treadmill.

Also, I never talked to those church members again! Not really; they are some of my closest friends. Thankfully they have not asked me to run another one.

One of my favorite events is watching Track and Field during the Olympics. Though I hate to run, there is still something impressive about watching athletes run. There is something about seeing someone run fast that is amazing. The way they move. Arms and legs are moving like a blur. Deep down, I wish I could do that. Nevertheless, I have decided to do other cardio things rather than run.

As we wrap up the last parable in Luke 15, we will see someone running. And just like the Olympics where runners are giving it their all, this is just as impressive, if not more so, when you know who is running and why!

A LONG WAY OFF

But when he came to himself, he said, 'How many of my father's hired servants have more than enough bread, but I perish here with hunger! I will arise and go to my father, and I will say to him, "Father, I have sinned against heaven and before you. I am no longer worthy to be called your son. Treat me as one of your hired servants."' And he arose and came to his father. But while he was still a long way off, his father saw him and felt compassion, and ran and embraced him and kissed him. (Luke 15:17-20)

It is incredible how much energy we expend during our lives based on what we earn and what we think we deserve. Have you ever got something, only to find out that someone you don't really like got something better? Suddenly, what you have is not good enough. This third parable of Jesus is based on this principle. Jesus is famous for giving people something that they don't deserve, and he usually gives it to them in front of people who are furious that Jesus did it.

Jesus says in Luke 15:11-12, "*There was a man who had two sons. And the younger of them said to his father, 'Father, give me the share of property that is coming to me.' And he divided his property between them.*" First off, in that culture, if a son said something like that to his dad, it would not only go wrong for the son, but it would also bring tremendous shame to that family. A son's property or inheritance doesn't come until the dad passes away. No son would ask that to his living dad. It was ridiculous. What is more outrageous is the dad said, okay.

Can you imagine what those pompous religious leaders thought when Jesus said this? What kind of dad would do this! This isn't a good dad; this is a bad dad. I would probably think this son was on drugs if this was me! No way will you get your inheritance while I am still living. You can forget your inheritance now; I will give it to your brother. Can you imagine what people will say to this? Do you understand the shame this will bring us if I do this? The gossip in that village would have blown up over this family.

"Hey! You hear about Jeremiah?"

"No, what about him?"

"Well, Josiah asked him for his inheritance early! And Jeremiah gave it to him!?

"No!"

"Yes!"

"What is it with this younger generation! I tell you what, if my sons did that to me, I would have one less son!"

"I know, right!"

Luke 15:13 says, "*Not many days later, the younger son gathered all he had and took a journey into a far country, and there he squandered his property in reckless living.*" OUCH! Not only did this son take his money early, but he blew it like he was on some kind of weekend bender in Las Vegas. Who is this kid? And to say he squandered his property would mean he traded it in for cash. You know, family heirlooms, stuff you really cannot put a price tag on. And he blows it all.

This parable is not pretty. It's ugly, and this son is not respectable at all. But it gets worse. He is now broke and hungry, so he tries to hire himself out to a pig farmer (a no-no in the Jewish culture) because the pig food is starting to look tasty. He is in a bad place. Even the sinners Jesus was eating with while he was telling this story probably thought this son was a train wreck.

Luke 15:17: "*But when he came to himself, he said, 'How many of my father's hired servants have more than enough bread, but I perish here with hunger!*" This young son is at the end of his rope. But I want you to think bigger than this son. There are so many people in our churches, neighborhoods, and maybe you are reading this right now, who are at rock bottom. Your life is not going so well. Maybe you lost your job and have been hard-pressed to find another one. Maybe your marriage is not where it should be. Maybe your kids are out of control, and you have no clue how to fix it. Maybe you are addicted to a certain sin, pulling you further away from God. You have hit rock bottom in some form or fashion, like this kid in the story. Can I just say hitting rock bottom may be the most important place you can find yourself in? All of us, when we hit rock bottom, the only thing we can say is, "I CANNOT!" I cannot do this anymore! I cannot overcome this by myself! I cannot find a way out! I CANNOT! Usually when we hit rock bottom, we being to realize that the only person who can get us out of the mess we found ourselves in is Jesus. And the beautiful thing about Jesus is not only CAN he get us out of it, but he WILL! He does it all the time!

Look at where this kid goes in his mind when he reaches rock bottom. "*I will arise and go to my father, and I will say to him, 'Father, I have sinned against heaven and before you. I am no longer worthy to be called your son. Treat me as one of your hired servants*" (Luke 15:18-19). Where does this kid's mind go? Back to his dad. Man, I would rather be just a regular employee at my dad's house than free, broken, and hungry somewhere else. Notice that this kid went from believing he earned his inheritance and having a place in his dad's house to feeling undeserving. I am so unworthy! I used to be worthy, but now—now I am not! Now, there is no way. I blew it! I cannot! How often do our lives revolve around how we should earn this or that and how we deserve this and that simply because we think we are good or better than others? This kid is no different from us.

"*And he arose and came to his father. But while he was still a long way off, his father saw him and felt compassion, and ran and embraced and kissed him*" (Luke 15:20). Here comes the train wreck. Here comes this kid who ran as far away from his father as he could go. Here comes this kid who spent everything his dad had worked for. Here comes this son who is so far away from being good. Have you ever felt that way? Have you ever felt so far away from being good? Maybe the person you are now is far from the person you know you should be. Have you ever felt like you are over here, but the man you know you should be is over there? Or you are over here, but the woman you should be is over there? Or you're here, but the spouse, parent, employee, or friend is a long way off from where you know you should be? Have you ever had those emotions or thoughts? Of course, who hasn't? All the while, sitting at rock bottom, we begin to prepare our speeches with Jesus, saying, I will get better. I promise. We come up with all kinds of plans to get better, all for the sake of trying to impress Jesus to earn or deserve his love.

I have thought about this, and it seems that I have been trying to fix things on my own in hopes of impressing Jesus for most of my Christian life. Saying things like: You watch Jesus; I will remedy this. I am going to stop this. I am going to start doing better. I will show you why I am not like those tax collectors and sinners. I will show you why I deserve it, how I can earn it, or why you should be proud of me! Looking back, not doubt heaven is shaking its head going, yeah, you are pretty much a train wreck; good luck trying to fix yourself. How is that coming along, by the way?

Truth hurts sometimes!

Have I ever come close to fixing myself? No. Have you? I mean, I am not even close. I am still a long way off. But then I think, well maybe tomorrow I will be better. Tomorrow, I promise, I will…

Stop, Scott! It never works!

This kid in the parable is just like us.

After all the speeches he was concocting in his head on how he would prove, earn, and deserve his father's love, the boy decided to go back home. Jesus says that the father saw his son first. Now, I can tell you what those Pharisees and scribes were thinking. They were thinking—yeah!—I bet this father saw his kid! No doubt this father had been looking for him because when he found him, he would let this boy have it! We will see an apocalyptic scolding unlike anything we have ever seen. This boy deserves nothing less. The dad is running because he is so angry at the son that he cannot wait another second before getting ahold of him to dropkick him and then put him in a chokehold! There will be no tap out for this kid! HOW DARE YOU SHAME ME!

Praise God, Jesus never said that. Of course, we would not have thought anything of it if he did. I mean, the boy deserved whatever punishment his father would dole out. After all, our nature is that if you did something hurtful to me, I would return the favor. You ruin me; I will destroy you. You forsake me; I will leave you. However, we need to remember that Jesus' love for us is irrational. When the dad sees the son, he has compassion for him.

Compassion?

On a not-so-good kid?

The story says that the dad ran to his son, hugged his neck, and kissed him. Say what? The audience had to be thinking that this story doesn't even make any sense. Before the kid could even say he was sorry, the dad was showering him as if it was Christmas morning. He was honoring him as if it was his twenty-first birthday. Bring out the best robe! Get the ring, put it on! Light up the grill and put the filet mignon on! Let's party! Everyone listening to Jesus explain this story had to be thinking this dad is a foolish, BAD dad! And the kid? Don't get me started on him. At the story's beginning, I didn't like this kid, and I sure don't like him now. This boy doesn't deserve all the love and fanfare his father is pouring out. But…

JESUS IS MY HERO BECAUSE HE RUNS TOWARDS ME IN COMPASSION EVEN WHEN I AM A LONG WAY OFF

It would be so much easier for us to understand this story if Jesus ended up getting mad or angry at us when we are a long way off from where we know we should be. Yet, he never does. Sure, he disciplines those he loves but gets mean or angry? Never! Why? Because our hero does the impossible. He loves us even when we are unlovable. He forgives us even when we should be unforgiven. He showers us with compassion even when we are hard of hearts. He comes running even when we are still a long way off. He is relentless.

When we look at the three parables in Luke 15, guess who we are in this story? We are the wandering sheep, the irrational coin, and the undeserving son. Jesus says I am the shepherd who will leave everything I have and go to the ends of the earth to find you when you wander. I am the woman who will irrationally and relentlessly turn everything upside down to find you. And I am the dad who will come running with compassion, even when you are a long way off from where you know you should be.

Jesus is our hero who runs! He runs toward the selfish. He runs toward the broken-hearted. He runs towards those who are incapable of fixing themselves. This is what he does! Without Jesus, we are just people who are broken and helpless to change ourselves. Have we not learned that by now? We all have wandered. We all have inconsistencies. We all have drifted away from the truth. We all have sinned, and will continue to keep on wandering. We all are prone to wander from the God we love. As much as we have tried over and over again, we still seem incapable of fixing ourselves. So often, we find ourselves a long way off.

Tell me, what did the sheep do to deserve Jesus' love? What did the coin do? Or the son? Nothing! They did absolutely nothing. The sheep would have kept wandering off. The coin would have remained where it was until it was found or forgotten altogether. The son, well, we can say he came back to his dad's house, but why? He ran out of money and was only coming back because he thought his dad might be gracious enough to hire him as an employee. No, the sheep, coin, and son did nothing to deserve or earn the compassion of Jesus, yet he gave it to them anyway. When will we realize that only one HERO comes running when our souls tend to drift? When are we going to realize that only Jesus has the compassion to come back for us time and time again when we lose sight of him? This is what Jesus does! He is a shepherd willing to risk everything for us because his love is irrational. He will always come running in his compassion, no matter how far off we have wandered! Jesus would quickly run a half marathon to come to find the ones who are still a long way off. And he would probably do it without even breaking a sweat or hurting his ankle. That is why he is my hero.

Something to Think About...

1. The parable of the lost son is about earning and deserving. If we earn it, we deserve it. If we don't earn it, then we don't deserve it. But this story, Jesus paints an extreme picture of how Jesus lavishly loves us despite whether we earn it or not. Why does Jesus love us so unconditionally?
2. Have you ever felt like the younger son where you did not deserve Jesus' love? Do you still feel that way, and if not, what changed?
3. The older son felt like he earned his father's love by always being obedient and serving. What was Jesus' response to this? How often do you think Christians keep track of all the good they do for Jesus? What is the fundamental flaw in this thinking?
4. Both sons are exhausted. One was exhausted by living recklessly, the other always trying to do good and earn his dad's love. Why can both ways of living ruin our relationship with Jesus?
5. How can this parable help us be a blessing to the people in our community and neighborhoods?

5

CHAPTER

Behold, A Leper Came

———◆———

WHO IS SAYING THESE THINGS

The Gospel of Matthew, chapters 8-12, is critical when it comes to understanding the life and message of Jesus Christ. During those chapters, Jesus performs a series of miracles followed by some teaching. No doubt there are countless miracles Jesus did during this time, but Matthew singles out nine of them. We will look at one of those miracles in this chapter. However, what is unfortunate is that after all these miracles and teaching moments, the religious leaders concluded that Jesus was just a sham. He was a fake. What was worse, they called Jesus an agent of the devil for loving and healing the oppressed and sick (Matt. 12:24). Jesus does all he can to show the world who he is, and in the end, they conclude he is the opposite of that.

In Matthew 7, we begin to see what is going on. Jesus just wrapped up the greatest sermon ever recorded in the Sermon on the Mount, and Matthew records, "*And when Jesus finished these sayings, the crowds were astonished at his teachings, for he was teaching them as one who had authority, and not as their scribes*" (Matthew 7:28-29).

The first question we should ask is how the scribes did it? If they were astonished by Jesus' teachings and it immediately reminded them that this is not how the scribes did it, then how did the scribes do it? For the most part, scribes were the theologians in Jesus' day. The Pharisees were the preachers and teachers, but the scribes were the theologians. The scribes were sometimes called rabbis in the Bible. Rabbi means "master" or "teacher," which I am sure was a title of honor that they loved to hear about themselves. However, as theologians, they were excellent at quoting from the rabbis of old. They were fallible people, so they needed many other fallible sources to support their teachings. Scribes were not given much to original thought. They had to back everything up with other sources. Not Jesus. He just said it, and he said it with unbelievable authority. In the process, Jesus was overturning their entire religious system. He was stripping these religious leaders naked.

This brings up another question. If we were first-century Jews, we would have to ask, "Who is this man saying these things?" I mean, honestly, who is this guy named Jesus, and by what authority is he saying these things. Or, more pointedly, by what right does he think he can say these things and then proclaim the truthfulness of his word without backing it up with any sources? Well, chapters eight and nine of the Gospel of Matthew answer this question.

Jesus will show without a shadow of a doubt that he is who he says he is. That he is indeed God himself and that he alone has the authority. How do we know he is God? We know because only God can create. So, for two chapters and nine examples, Jesus creates situations out of nothing. He will create circumstances that don't exist. He will create limbs that were not there before. He will create life when it was previously dead. He will create calm during a storm. He will create healings that were utterly incurable. He created situations that were otherwise not there. Only God can do that. From the beginning, Matthew wants us to see that Jesus will establish his authority through miracles and compassion for those at the deepest level of need. Unfortunately, at the end of chapter 12, they still won't believe Jesus is, in fact, God.

I have heard many people tell me that they wish that Jesus would do more miracles today as he did when he walked this earth. Don't get me wrong; I wish Jesus would do more miracles in our time but look how it ended in Jesus' day. At the end of the Gospel of John, John states that if he could have written all the things Jesus did, the *world itself could not contain the books that would be written"* (John 21:25). I mean, it was miracle after miracle. He was healing one after the other. And yet, they still did not believe. Suppose Jesus was here today, doing what only he can do. In that case, I am sure many would just write off his miracles as natural or scientific phenomena. I can imagine that Matthew 12 must have been a saddening time for Jesus when they still don't believe after everything he has done.

Matthew chapter 8 begins where Matthew chapter 4 ends, with the Sermon on the Mount thrown in the middle. At the end of Matthew 4, Matthew says:

> *And he went throughout all Galilee, teaching in their synagogues and proclaiming the gospel of the kingdom and healing every disease and every affliction among the people. So his fame spread throughout all Syria, and they brought him all the sick, those afflicted with various diseases and pains, those oppressed by demons, those having seizures, and paralytics, and he healed them. And great crowds followed him from Galilee and the Decapolis, and from Jerusalem and Judea, and from beyond the Jordan.* (Matthew 4:23-25)

Jesus is just going from place to place doing all these miracles and healings. Shortly after this, he goes up to a mountainside and preaches the Sermon on the Mount, and then he heads back down the mountain to continue doing what he was doing before. Thousands upon uncounted thousands of healings. He healed all who came to him without preference, which is what we will see when we go to Matthew 8.

> *When he came down from the mountain, great crowds followed him. And behold, a leper came to him and knelt before him, saying, "Lord, if you will, you can make me clean." And Jesus stretched out his hand and touched him, saying, "I will; be clean." And immediately his leprosy was cleansed. And Jesus said to him, "See that you say nothing to anyone, but go, show yourself to the priest and offer the gift that Moses commanded, for a proof to them.* (Matthew 8:1-4)

This is a very well-known story. More than likely, you have heard this story before. For most, we read this and go, "Ah! Isn't that just nice! Nice story. Poor leper! I bet he was thankful Jesus healed him." However, what I want to do from this story is to show you one of the greatest reasons why Jesus is my hero.

HANSEN'S DISEASE

"Behold a leper came to him" (Matt 8:1). The word "came" in Greek means to approach. This is an interesting word Matthew uses because, in that culture, lepers don't approach anyone! Ever! Do you know anything about lepers? Lepers come from the Greek word *lepas*, which means scale or scaly. It means the same thing in Hebrew. It's some kind of visible scaly skin disease. At least the skin is a part of the disease. It is what we call Hansen's disease today. Dr. Gerhard Henrick Armauer Hansen, a scientist from Norway, noticed that a germ caused leprosy and not a sin or a curse (the prevalent thinking for the longest time). The Leprosy Mission International stated that leprosy is a disease "found most commonly in places of poverty" where poor nutrition means that "people's immune systems are not strong and they are less able to fight the disease."[1] Scientist will say that around 95% of the world is naturally immune to leprosy; however, it is still prevalent in South America and India.

Some scholars claim that leprosy originated in Egypt because they found the disease in an excavated mummified person dating back to the 4th century.[2] If this is true, then we can assume that the children of Israel picked up this disease when they were in captivity there. Regardless of where it originated, we know it was a problem in Moses' day.

As God instructed his people on how to live, God gave Israel many laws. Some of those laws were to protect the Israelites from plagues and diseases. One of those laws was on leprosy.

Leviticus 13:1-3 says:

> *The Lord spoke to Moses and Aaron, saying, "When a person has on the skin of his body a swelling or an eruption or a spot, and it turns into a case of leprous disease on the skin of his*

body, then he shall be brought to Aaron the priest or to one of his sons the priests, and the priest shall examine the diseased area on the skin of his body. And if the hair in the diseased area has turned white and the disease appears to be deeper than the skin of his body, it is a case of leprous disease. When the priest has examined him, he shall pronounce him unclean.

After God instructs the priests on what to do with such a person, he then adds:

The leprous person who has the disease shall wear torn clothes and let the hairs of his head hang loose, and he shall cover his upper lip and cry out, 'Unclean, unclean.' He shall remain unclean as long as he has the disease. He is unclean. He shall live alone. His dwelling shall be outside the camp. (Leviticus 13:45-46)

I think to a certain degree, especially after all we went through with the COVID-19 pandemic back in 2020, with all the lockdowns, masks, and social distancing, we can grasp the severity of the stigma of this disease. Nevertheless, I am not sure we can fully get the isolation and complete loneliness they have gone through. Sure, we went through a couple of months where we stayed home and didn't interact with people, and if we had to go out, we purposely tried staying six feet apart and covered our faces as we went. But we had Facetime, Twitter, and other social media at our disposal where we could continue to interact with our friends and loved ones. Not so with lepers. I mean, here is a man or a woman who, for the rest of their lives, has to cover their face and shout out "UNCLEAN! UNCLEAN!" everywhere they went. Leviticus 12:46 commanded that they live alone. According to the Jewish historian Josephus, lepers lived alone and were expelled from the city entirely.[3] So, alone and isolated. That's a deadly combination. The Talmud proclaimed that anyone with leprosy had to stay 6 feet away from other people and 150 feet if it was windy outside.[4] So, if you were wondering where the original six feet social distancing originated, now you know.

Thankfully, today we can somewhat control it and have a slightly normal life, but it was utterly uncontrollable and incurable back then.

To understand why Jesus is our hero, we need to understand a bit of what leprosy does. The fundamental issue with leprosy is that it attacks. It attacks your nervous system making your limbs go numb. This numbness is the primary reason why limbs such as hands and feet begin to fall off. To be honest, it is not that their hands and feet just one day fall off, but because they cannot feel their limbs, they end up rubbing them off. It attacks your muscles which can cause paralysis, leading to "clawed hands" where your fingers deteriorate and curl up, or "foot drop" where your feet are no longer functioning normally, and you limp or drag your feet as you walk.[5] It attacks your bone marrow, affecting your blood supply, making your bones begin to wither and your skin draw close to the bones, making you look deathly. It attacks the eyes, which brings blindness. Because of the paralysis of the eyelids, you cannot close your eyes or even blink. It attacks your hair, making it fall out, including your eyebrows and eyelashes. It attacks your larynx, which gives your voice a grating, rough, six-packs-of-cigarettes-a-day type of voice. Thankfully it is not that painful because you lose all feelings. Still, when you include the sores, puss, spots, and deformities all over your body, it is the most horrific and ugliest thing imaginable in the world. This disease brought fear in Jesus' day, and rightly so. Luke will also tell us that there were many lepers in Israel (Luke 4:27). To make matters worse, there was no cure for leprosy.

Add to the insult of living with this incurable sickness; leprosy ended up becoming the most graphic illustration of what sin is. In other words, when people in Jesus' day would see a leper, they would associate that person with sin. Sin, as we all know, defiles the whole body. Sin is ugly. Sin is incurable. Sin is disgusting. It's disfiguring. Sin separates, alienates, and makes men and women outcasts. Every leper not only had to live with the stigma of this disease, but they also had to live with being a walking illustration of the devastation of what sin does. As you can imagine, people hated them simply because they represented sin. When people saw or heard a leper screaming out, "UNCLEAN!" they despised them merely because they feared them. Which makes this story in the Gospel of Matthew interesting to me because it was with a leper that Jesus began to show his authority to the world.

BEHOLD A LEPER CAME

Now we know why the word "behold" is there. Behold means, WHAT THE WHAT!! CAN YOU BELIEVE THIS! NO WAY!

Behold, a leper came!

Behold, a leper approached.

Look, lepers don't approach. That is forbidden. It is unthinkable. It's not just personal humiliation and a social stigma, but it is an Old Testament law. The Old Testament made it clear that you could not approach anyone if you had leprosy. Lepers don't approach people. They just went around mumbling, stumbling, covering themselves up, constantly repeating "unclean, unclean." Social distancing wasn't something new we created in 2020 with COVID-19; it was forever a way of life for these people. However, there must have been something about Jesus and his reputation that drew the unthinkable to him.

With boldness, this man approached Jesus, and I can imagine how fast that crowd would have parted. You could just hear the gasps as he walked toward Jesus. Luke will add that this man was full of leprosy (Luke 5:12). It means he didn't have to scream out "unclean" because the people would easily have noticed that this man was full of this disease. But what did he care? As far as his reputation is concerned, he didn't have any, so who cares if people were upset that he disturbed their precious little lives by walking in their midst. Here was a man who recognized his need to be whole so desperately that he couldn't care less what people thought or even what the Old Testament said about leprosy.

He knew the misery of shame and desolation of his isolation. He knew what it was like to be an outcast. Who cares if one more law of the Old Testament was broken? It's not as if he can be broken any more than he was right then. So, he approached.

"Lord, if you will, you can make me clean" (Matt 8:2). I like that. This leper didn't come with demands as to why he should be healed. He didn't even try to ascribe to Jesus his own worthiness to be healed. Nothing was brought up on how he drew the short straw and how it was totally unfair that he got this disease while all his other buddies and loved ones didn't. He didn't talk about his rights. He didn't even talk about his desires. He didn't even say he would like to be healed. He just said, "Jesus, I don't know

if you want to heal me or not, and that is solely up to you, but if you want to, I know you can."

"If you will." In Greek, it's the word *dunamis*, which we get the word dynamite from. It means power. This lonely man in the suffering state of leprosy came to Jesus and said, "I don't know if you will do this or not, but what I do know is that you have the power to heal me if you want to. I know that. I am convinced of that." Maybe this man had complete faith in who Jesus was. Perhaps he knew something that the thousands of people surrounding Jesus at that time didn't. One thing is clear, everything about this man lets us know that he believed Jesus could do it. He didn't know if he would do it, but he was convinced that he could do it if he wanted to, which shows how great this man's faith was. Jesus, I know you can, but whatever happens here, it will be your choice, not mine. That takes some faith!

Matt 8:3: *"And Jesus stretched out his hand and touched him, saying, 'I will; be clean.' And Immediately his leprosy was cleansed."* Jesus reached out and touched this man—this man in the full stages of leprosy!

Ummm...gross!

Sometimes you got to love what the Bible doesn't say because I can imagine what happened the moment Jesus did this. Everyone and I mean everyone, probably lost it, including his disciples. Maybe a couple of older ladies passed out. Can you imagine growing up where leprosy was numerous in your town? You went to the mall, and people with leprosy were at the entrance begging for money or food. People under the overpasses, full of leprosy, begging for scraps and handouts. Everywhere you went, someone had leprosy. And to top that off, you were told from a very early age that leprosy was a picture of sin. I can hear my mom yelling at me:

"Who stole a cookie from the cookie jar? Scott, was it you? I know it was!"

"No, Mom, I promise it wasn't me!" (As I wipe the chocolate from my face and the crumbs from my clothes).

"Do you know that God hates it when we lie? Do you know that God hates it when we steal? Do you want to get leprosy because that is what happens when you sin!"

Yeah, that would make me think twice before I snagged another cookie from the pantry! Well, probably not. Cookies are my kryptonite!

Leprosy, sin. Sin, leprosy. They were both interchangeable back then. You don't touch lepers! But, do you want to know what lepers needed more than anything else in the entire world? They needed to be touched. In the full stage of this disease, this man has not been touched by another human in maybe years. Can you imagine that? Can you imagine not being touched by another human for years? No holding hands. No kissing. No hugs. No physical contact at all. I honestly cannot imagine that, and when I try to, it's like my mind shuts me down because to think of such a thing hurts my soul.

Jesus touched him.

The amazing thing is that Jesus didn't have to. I mean, we know Jesus well enough now to see that he could have quickly healed him with just a word and that man would have been clean without ever being touched. He could have stood back the customary social distance of six feet, stretched out his arms, and healed him. The heavens would have exploded, the angels would have sung their praises, and the people surrounding Jesus would have golf-clapped and celebrated, and that would be it. But that is not Jesus' style. He touched him, and immediately he was healed.

I love the simplicity in this.

For me, one of the greatest proofs that the Bible is divine is the writers' simplicity and lack of commentary. If you or I were writing this story, we would have written about twenty pages worth explaining this event because of what an event it was. I would have written something like this: "The moment we saw this despicable of all creatures coming towards our Lord, we were petrified. We were frozen in place. How could this sinful creature approach the purest of all beings? The crowd all around was immobile in fear, not knowing what to do or where to go. It happened so fast. At one moment, we were all laughing it up at a joke Jesus was saying about three Pharisees walking into a bar, and the next moment this—this—*monster*—was in our midst. Lydia, the lady standing next to me, screamed a blood-curdling screech that about blew out my eardrums, and then she passed out. Joseph gasped out loud, then took off like a gazelle back up the mountainside where Jesus had just wrapped up a great sermon. The audacity of this leper! But then, to the amazement of us all, Jesus, as if in slow motion, reached out his hand. Time stood still. The wind stopped blowing. The birds stopped chirping. Jesus begins to extend his hand to touch the untouchable, the vilest of all creations. And as his hand was stretched out...."

Nope, none of that.

I will.

Be clean.

Immediately he was healed of his leprosy. Probably one of the greatest proofs that the Bible is divinely written is the lack of all that fanfare.

Now, I am not sure what happened, but I can guess. The moment that Jesus said, "be clean," this man's shriveled up hands were made whole again. His feet beautiful. His face unmarred and restored. His paralysis, healed. His hair, fully grown. His bones, strong again. His eyelids, back to blinking. Instantly whole.

JESUS IS MY HERO BECAUSE NO MATTER WHO YOU ARE OR WHAT YOU HAVE BECOME, JESUS IS ALWAYS APPROACHABLE

The whole point of this story, and for that matter, why Jesus came to earth, is to let us know that he is always approachable. Always. So often, our lives are messy, and life plays no favorites. All of us hurt. All of us feel moments of loss. All of us wonder how in the world we're going to overcome this obstacle in front of us. All of us, at times, question the meaning and purpose of our lives. And Jesus knows that about us. And still, he will always be approachable in those moments.

Maybe you are reading this right now, and you are like this leper. To be honest, there is a reason why leprosy illustrates the power of sin in our lives. So maybe you are reading this, and you are like this leper where you are struggling with some type of sin in your life. A sin that is ugly. A sin that is loathsome. A sin that is incurable and can easily make you an outcast to society.

Jesus is approachable.

Maybe you are living in fear. Fear of being ostracized. Fear of being caught or found out. Fear of the future. Fear of the present. Fear of the past catching up to you. Fear of being disliked. Learn from this leper and lose all fear of being banished, hated, or despised. Right here, right now, say I don't care anymore. I need help because, honestly, I am so overwhelmed right now; I am not sure I can do this another day!

Jesus is approachable.

This leper came in humility and knelt at Jesus' feet. The word knelt (Matthew 8:2) is the Greek verb *proskenein* and is a word that is only used when describing worship to God. It represents a person's feeling and action of worship in the presence of the divine. This leper not only came to Jesus in humility, but he worshipped him. Maybe you are spiritually bankrupt. Perhaps it has been a while since you enjoyed worshiping Jesus. Could it be that somewhere down the line, we lost sight of the fact that our souls are the most important and that only Jesus can bring satisfaction to our souls. Go to him. He is always available.

Jesus is approachable.

The leper came in faith. And maybe that is the hardest part for you. Our world is an ugly mistress and all of us, if we are not careful, can become tainted by it. We lose faith in people. We lose faith in ourselves. We lose faith in family, or just as worse, we lose faith in our church family. Ultimately, we can lose faith in Jesus. Jeremiah said it best when he said, *"The heart is deceitful above all things, and desperately sick; who can understand it?"* (Jeremiah 17:9). No doubt, this leper was tempted to lose faith in people and in himself. He probably was told thousands of times that his heart was deceitful and desperately sick, which is why he got leprosy in the first place while others did not. How easy do you think it could have been for this leper to lose faith in himself and see himself as despicable and ugly? How easy do you think it would have been to lose faith in the people around him, especially since everyone shunned him, probably called him names at best, or tormented and inflicted pain on him at worst? He wasn't allowed in the church because of this disease, so losing faith in God could have been easy. But he didn't. He didn't let the world get him down. He didn't let people's words dishearten him and send him to a dark, desolate place. He didn't let his isolation and loneliness be the blanket that covered his spirit and soul. No! He had faith that Jesus could make him whole again. He had faith that there was someone worth believing again, a hero worth following again. So, he came to the only one he knew could get him out of the rut and mire and mud he found himself in. He came to Jesus. Why?

Jesus is approachable.

Do you believe that Jesus is approachable? Do you believe that he can do the unthinkable in your life? I know about Jesus that he is willing and able to turn my whole life around when it is going in the wrong direction. He is always approachable and willing to meet me where I am. Trust me; he has had to turn me around too many times to count. Reread the Gospels!

How many times do we have to read that Jesus never turned anyone away? How many times do we read that Jesus healed and made everyone whole? He brought wholeness to everyone he ever met. Did Jesus know that the majority of those he came to bring wholeness would turn their backs on him and walk away? Sure he did. But do you want to know something about my hero? He never turned them away! Why?

Jesus is approachable.

No matter where you are in life right now, no matter the sins you find yourself in or the troubles you face, no matter how tough life can get and how frustrated you become at things and people, Jesus will always be approachable. Jesus longs for us to approach him. He longs for you to come to him. He longs to reach out, touch you, and bring healing and wholeness to your life. He craves it! It brings him delight because he desires fellowship and friendship with you. Do not ever forget that no matter what you are going through, no matter what sin you find yourself committing or who you have become our hero is always present, always accessible, and always approachable. What a hero we have in Jesus!

Something to Think About...

1. In Leviticus 13 and 14, God instructs the priests on recognizing leprosy and isolating the disease. Nowhere in the Bible is there any mention of how to cure leprosy. Only God Himself could cleanse the leper. With that in mind, why did Jesus choose to cure this leper, and what does this prove about Jesus?

2. This is the first time in the Gospels where anyone called Jesus "lord." What is the significance of seeing Jesus as Lord? What makes Jesus your Lord?

3. How important is social status to you? After reading this parable, how important is social status to Jesus? Why do you think we make it more important than Jesus does?

4. How does knowing that Jesus is always approachable mean to you no matter what you have done or become?

5. How often do you approach Jesus with the everyday things in your life? And if not, why not?

6

CHAPTER

It's Okay To Interrupt

❖━━━◆◆◆━━━❖

INTERRUPTION MALFUNCTION

I hate to be interrupted. It doesn't matter if it is my wife, children, friends, or whomever. I don't like to be distracted when I am in the middle of something. I am sure you can agree with me. Most of us hate to be interrupted when we are engrossed in something. There are only two people I have ever met who were okay with interruptions in their lives: moms and my buddy, Jay Johnson.

As for moms, I am not sure I have ever met a mom who didn't take interruptions with a grain of salt. You have a mom busy doing something, and suddenly kids come running like a bat out of H. E. Double Hockey Sticks, needing something and wanting something. Must have something.

Hey Mom!

Hey Mom!

Hey Mom!

MOM!!

They don't care that mom is busy working on the spreadsheet due in two hours for her company. They don't care if mom is busy cleaning. They don't care if mom is busy cooking. They don't care if mom is using the bathroom. They don't care that mom is working on the last chapter of her Doctorate.

They don't care.

At all.

Ever.

Moms, I honestly don't know how you do it. Your lack of losing control and killing a child amid all the interruptions they cause during a single 24-hour period is genuinely inspirational. I am sure if I were in your position, I would be in prison by now.

My buddy, Jay Johnson, is the other person who doesn't care about interruptions. I met him when I was in 10th grade. He sat in front of me during my first-period class, and he was easy to notice since most of his left leg was bandaged up with blood and ooze seeping out. I couldn't help it; I leaned forward and asked, "Hey, what happened to your leg?" He replied he got hurt by a three-wheeler. Keep in mind that this was back in the '90s when three-wheelers were the norm for off-road shenanigans. Jay was going a little too fast and flipped his three-wheeler. He ended up getting stuck underneath it while the hot muffler fried his leg like bacon on a griddle and gave him severe burns. These types of injuries were relatively standard with three-wheelers, and that is one of the reasons you now have four-wheelers (quads, to the enthusiasts out there), where their suspensions are much more stable and less likely to flip. Unfortunately for Jay, they were not invented yet, so now he started his 10th-grade looking like a half mummy.

As I got to know Jay better, we became fast friends. He was cool, laid back, loyal, and didn't care about being popular. This was a breath of fresh air because 10th grade is where you are supposed to sell your soul to the devil so you can be the cool kid in school. Not Jay. He was just the same easy-going Jay no matter where he went. Whether you liked him or not, he didn't really care.

When it came to his friends, he would give the shirt off his back. Literally. I saw him do it one time when a buddy ripped his shirt. Jay took off his shirt, tossed it to him, and said, "Here, wear mine." He went the rest of the day without a shirt and not a care in the world.

His friends were the world to him, and no interruptions or distractions would take his mind off his buddies when they were together. I remember a time during a break at college when I went to visit him. I practically lived in his parent's double-wide trailer when I was in high school, so I just walked on in. I hadn't seen him in about a year, and I saw his bathroom door open, and he was in the middle of shaving his face. When he saw me, he smiled and gave me the biggest hug. I told him I was going to take him out to lunch and headed outside the bathroom to let him finish up and went to say hello to his mom.

As we were sitting at the restaurant, I noticed something was wrong with his face. At first, I couldn't figure it out, but when I looked closer, I noticed that only one side of his face was shaved smooth, and the other had about a 48-hour growth to it.

"Jay?"

"What?"

"Bro, did you forget to shave the other side of your face?"

"Oh! Yeah—well—when you came over, you surprised me, and I quit shaving so we could hang out."

"You quit shaving so we could hang out? You know I would have waited so you could finish up?"

"Sure, but who cares. I'm just glad you are here. Let's eat."

That's Jay! You interrupt Jay with what he is doing, and he will stop immediately and focus on you.

Another time we were driving somewhere late at night, and my future wife, Charlotte, was in the car with us. Charlotte and I were about three months into our relationship, so this was the crucial period where I did all I could to impress her into thinking I was someone I'm usually not. As we were driving, Jay noticed a car on the side of the road. I think Charlotte and I were gazing lovingly into each other's eyes because I never saw that vehicle.

Jay insisted we should pull over and help this guy. I don't know about you, but I have never felt comfortable pulling over at night to help a deserted stranger. Maybe I am not as Christlike as Jay because I would have said, "stinks for you!" and kept on driving. No way I was going to be interrupted by some strange man on the side of the road at night. Nope. Keep on driving.

Not Jay.

Jay turned the car around, and as we were pulling up, I noticed a truck was flipped on its side in the grass by the road. A man in his 30's, with a cigarette on his lips, stood by the truck and watched us as we approached. I asked Charlotte to stay in the car, and Jay and I got out to see if we could lend this guy a helping hand. Apparently, this guy had been drinking as his breath stank of it, and every other word was slurred. He's barely able to walk or stand still which might have been another giveaway, but whatever.

"Hey, you okay? You need any help?"

"My trip flucked."

"You're what?"

"I said, my trip flucked!"

"Say what?

"I said, my truck flipped!"

"Oh, gotcha. I can see that. What happened?"

"I slaw this rabbit. Biggum too. Ran right out in front of me. Tried to get it. Missed. Ended up here."

"Sure you did. Well, do you need us to call someone and get you some help?"

"Nah, trucks fine. Help me flip it back, and we should be good to go."

Now, I don't know about you, but I was still a buck thirty-five soaking wet. Never did gain that freshman fifteen in college. I could barely flip over a rabbit, let alone a two thousand pound truck. Jay was not much more than me. But Jay looked at Drunk Ted and replied, "Alright, let's do this."

Sure enough, and to my complete amazement, we flipped the truck back over on its side. I am not sure how it happened; maybe Drunk Ted had superhuman drunk strength, but we all pushed and grunted, and after a minute, that truck flipped back over and righted itself. D.T. got in the truck, cranked it right up, gave us each a fist bump, and then took off looking for more rabbits to kill.

Charlotte saw the whole thing. So, when we climbed up in Jay's vehicle, I couldn't help but say, "Did you see us flip that truck!" I mean, I haven't proposed yet, so anything I could do to impress my girl, I would. No doubt, this demonstrative display of utter strength would win me some points. She looked at me as seriously as she could and replied, "It was a small truck."

I almost dumped her right then!

Have you ever seen anyone who doesn't mind interruptions? I haven't met many. In this next story, one little interruption changed the course of a woman's life forever, and thankfully the man who was interrupted didn't mind the distraction at all.

And when Jesus had crossed again in the boat to the other side,
a great crowd gathered about him, and he was beside the sea.
Then came one of the rulers of the synagogue, Jairus by name,

and seeing him, he fell at his feet and implored him earnestly, saying, "My little daughter is at the point of death. Come and lay your hands on her, so that she may be made well and live." And he went with him. And a great crowd followed him and thronged about him. And there was a woman who had had a discharge of blood for twelve years, and who had suffered much under many physicians, and had spent all that she had, and was no better but rather grew worse. She had heard the reports about Jesus and came up behind him in the crowd and touched his garment. For she said, "If I touch even his garments, I will be made well." And immediately the flow of blood dried up, and she felt in her body that she was healed of her disease. And Jesus, perceiving in himself that power had gone out from him, immediately turned about in the crowd and said, "Who touched my garments?" And his disciples said to him, "You see the crowd pressing around you, and yet you say, 'Who touched me?'" And he looked around to see who had done it. But the woman, knowing what had happened to her, came in fear and trembling and fell down before him and told him the whole truth. And he said to her, "Daughter, your faith has made you well; go in peace, and be healed of your disease" (Mark 5:21-34).

BEING AVAILABLE

One of the most significant reasons why Jesus is my hero is because he is always approachable. Jesus is not like most leaders who live in the McMansions, with their privacy fences and security, doing all they can to seclude themselves from people. Jesus spent the entirety of his ministry in public. He didn't care if he encountered people in the streets or on the highway or hillside. He would meet people in the fields, homes, and synagogues. And in this story, he was pressed all around by people near the sea. You will only find a few occasions where Jesus would withdraw to spend some alone time to pray to God the Father or to speak privately to his disciples. But he would always go back to the people. Always. Jesus was very approachable, and as a result, he became a celebrity-like figure, like Robin Hood.

When you look at this story, though, two heroic things are revealed about Jesus. First...

JESUS IS MY HERO BECAUSE HE IS ALWAYS AVAILABLE WHEN I NEED HIM THE MOST

Here comes this man named Jairus, who has a sick 12-year-old daughter. He manages to push his way through the crowds and speak to Jesus. Praise God, Jesus is approachable. "My daughter is sick. Can you come to my house and heal her?" And verse 24 says, *"And he went with him"* (Mark 5:24).

I believe it is one thing to be always approachable, but it is another to be always available. To be available goes a little bit deeper. When Jesus is approachable, it means you can get near him, touch him, have contact with him, and be spoken to by him. But being always available means he is willing to give himself up for you. He will give you his time, energy, and attention solely to you. His availability means he doesn't have a problem dropping everything he is doing to be with you.

Here we see a man approach Jesus and declare his wish for him to come to his house and heal his daughter, and Jesus doesn't even think. He drops everything and walks off with this man. No doubt it may have been an effort to leave the crowds and be available to this one man. Everyone who approaches Jesus wants to see Jesus and spend time with him too, but Jesus is not like everyone else. He will always make time for you in moments of great need. He is always available.

I am reminded of what Jesus said in Matthew 12:20, *"A bruised reed he will not break, and a smoldering wick he will not quench."* Jesus, quoting from Isaiah 42:3, is saying that whenever he encounters someone who is bruised, battered, or hurting, or in desperate need of help, when the flame is about to go out in their life or when all light is fading and there is not much hope left, Jesus will do all he can to be available to that person making sure that he doesn't do anything to let that person down further. He will never blow out that smoldering wick. He is available. And in his availability, he will go with you to provide you with some respite, rest, and restoration. I love that about Jesus! Yes, he is my hero not only because he is approachable, but also because he is always available in times of need.

Don't ever forget that Jesus is available to you. There is never a time in your life when Jesus is too busy to spend time with you. There is never a time in your life when things are not going well, and Jesus is too busy to help. There is never a time when Jesus is too tired to lift his weary hands to help. No, he never gets tired. He never gets weary. He never gets fatigued. He is unlike anyone you will ever meet!

Jesus is always available to you. Do you believe that? Do you believe that his availability has no strings attached? Do you believe that Jesus' availability is like his mercy where it is new every morning? Because he is always present in your life, and he is always available to you when you need him the most. He is available when you just need someone to talk to. He is available when you need counsel. He is available when you need rest. He is available when you are searching for a purpose. He is available when you need healing. He is available when you long not to be alone. He is available when you cannot find your way out of a situation. He is always available.

Always.

Don't ever forget that!

There is, however, another side of this story that makes Jesus even more heroic. Yes, he is approachable. Yes, he is available. But third...

JESUS IS MY HERO BECAUSE HE IS DOESN'T MIND ME INTERRUPTING HIM WHEN I NEED HIM

Imagine this scene with me. Jesus couldn't even leave the beach because of all the people. He is always approachable. Finally, this man Jairus makes his way to Jesus, pleads with him to come to his house to heal his daughter because she is gravely sick, and Jesus heads off with this man. Jesus is always available. But as he was moving towards Jairus' house, a woman enters the scene and completely interrupts Jesus. "Hey Jesus, can you help my daughter? She is sick!" Immediately, Jesus goes with this man. However, as they walk to the man's house, instantly Jesus stops. Something is not right. Someone touched him. Someone else was in dire need.

Praise God for a hero who is willing to be interrupted!

They are an interesting duo when you think about these two people, Jairus and the woman. They have no relationship with each other, as far as we can tell. Still, both are brought together because of our hero Jesus. One was a man, the other a woman. One was well off; the other was poor. One is a respected leader in the community; the other is a rejected outcast. One is privileged; the other is repressed. One leads a synagogue; the other has been excommunicated from the synagogue. One has a twelve-year-old daughter who is dying, and the other has a twelve-year-old disease that is killing her.

Both are suffering and in need of a hero.

Jairus' daughter has reached the age where girls were soon married off. Yeah, I know! Thank God we don't abide by those customs anymore. My daughter is fourteen, and all the boys I see around here are complete fools who don't know the difference between mortgage and moron. No way I would offer my daughter to any of those boys! But back then, this was supposed to be an anticipated time in a girl's life for marriage. It should be filled with joyful excitement, and expectation. But she is sick. And if you keep reading Mark 5, it says in verse 35, that she dies.

On the other hand, you have the woman—who completely interrupts Jesus, I might add—and she has had some kind of bleeding for the last twelve years. She has had a hemorrhage that had lasted as long as Jairus' daughter has been alive. We don't know what caused it, but we can easily assume that this much blood loss would lead to severe bodily issues, not to mention loss of strength. But more than that, according to Leviticus 15, any woman with any kind of bleeding issue would be considered ceremonially unclean. This means for the last twelve years, this woman was unclean. She couldn't go to the synagogue to worship. This woman couldn't worship or have fellowship with believers for the last twelve years.

If she had a husband and touched him, he was unclean. If she had children and she touched them, they were unclean. If she touched a friend, they were unclean. According to Leviticus 15, if she touched anything and someone came behind her and touched it, they became unclean. If you think you have had it bad, you have no clue how much worse this woman has had. Can you imagine living a life like that? No hugs. No kisses. No touch from anyone. It had to have been unbearable. She was an outcast, ceremonially, ritually, unclean. Her entire community had rejected her.

This woman was like the leper, becoming a walking illustration of sinfulness. Not only was she physically ill, constantly unclean, and regarded as an outcast, but every waking moment she was a walking reminder of sinfulness. There was nothing she could do to rise above that.

JEWISH TASSELS

She had heard the reports about Jesus and came up behind him in the crowd and touched his garment. For she said, "If I touch even his garments, I will be made well." And immediately the flow of blood dried up, and she felt in her body that she was healed of her disease (Mark 5:27-29).

This passage is remarkable, but when you understand what is going on in the Jewish context, this passage becomes even more powerful. This woman not only knew her Bible—despite not being able to worship in the synagogue—but she also believed that Jesus was the Messiah. Let me explain.

In the book of Numbers, God instructs all the people of Israel to make tassels (*tzitzityot*) on the corners (*kanaph*) of their garments (Numbers 15:37-39)[1]. The desire here was that all the people of Israel would wear these tassels. They would be a constant reminder of the commandments of God and that hopefully, as they wear them and look at them, they will remember and obey. I can imagine one of the Israelites going up to Moses and saying:

"You are telling us that God wants us to wear these tassels that we have attached to our outer garments?"

"Yes."

"Umm…Every day?"

"Yes."

"Even when we go to the grocery store to buy food?"

"Yes."

"Even when we go to church?"

"Yes."

"Okay, what about when we are plowing in the fields or tending to our sheep?"

"Yes."

"Okay, last one. What about when we go to the gym and sweat all over the place?

"Yes."

"Really? Do you want us to wear these robes with tassels even when we are hot and sweaty? Why?"

"Because whenever you see them. Whenever they get all dirty or bother you, or whenever you notice them, God wants us to remember that He gave us, and all the people of Israel, six hundred and thirteen commandments to live by and that we will obey them."

Basically, God wants all the people of Israel to wear a visual aid to remind them of God's commandments. It was a reminder of God's love for them and how God would forever protect them if they were obedient to God and his commandments. So, all the people of Israel wore these tassels everywhere they went.

We also need to understand that the Hebrew language is considered a poor language. Poor, not in the sense that it is bad, but poor in the sense that it does not have a lot of words. For example, the English language has about 175,000 words, not including 50,000 words that have become obsolete. (My wife uses about 150,000 of those words...every...single... day!) The Hebrew language, on the other hand, has around 33,000 words. What makes the Hebrew language beautiful (or frustrating, depending on if you were forced to learn Hebrew in your MDiv degree!) is that many words have multiple meanings.[2]

When God said to put tassels on the corners (*kanaph*) of their garments, the word for the corner has multiple meanings. It can mean corner, as in the corner of a table, but it also means wings, as in a bird's wing.

> "*The LORD repay you for what you have done, and a full reward be given you by the LORD, the God of Israel, under whose wings* (kanaph) *you have come to take refuge*" (Ruth 2:12).

> "*Keep me as the apple of your eye; hide me in the shadow of your wings* (kanaph)" (Psalms 17:8).

"How precious is your steadfast love, O God! The children of mankind take refuge in the shadows of your wings (kanaph)" (Psalms 36:7).

"For you have been my help, and in the shadow of your wings (kanaph) I will sing to you" (Psalms 63:7).

Over and over again, the Bible paints this picture of God protecting his people by covering them or protecting them with the shadow of his wings. The Israelites believed that if they attached these tassels to the corner of their robes and faithfully remembered God's commandments, they would be under the shadow and the protection of his wings. So, every Jewish person would sew these tassels on their garments and walk around everywhere as they dangled in the breeze.

This picture becomes more evident when you think of King Saul and young David in 1 Samuel 24. David, at this time, had already been promised by God to be the king of Israel. On the other hand, Saul went a little cray-cray and is now seeking to kill David so he can remain on the throne. David had to flee from the presence of Saul, and in 1 Samuel 24, we find David and his men hiding out in a cave. King Saul decided to visit them as they were taking some shelter from the hot middle eastern sun. Now, Saul did not know David was in the cave, and David had no clue Saul was coming. Saul just wanted to use the bathroom. When David's men knew who walked into the cave, they approached David and said, "Now is the time to kill Saul and take your rightful place on the throne" (1 Samuel 24:4-5).

David sneaks up to Saul, but he cuts off a corner of Saul's robe instead of killing him. What's on the corner of Saul's robe? Saul may have lost his mind and become a jealous king, but he is still Jewish. So what is on the corner of his robe? His tassels. When he cut off the corner with the tassels on Saul's robe, what was David saying? In effect, he was saying that Saul is no longer under the shadow and protection of God's wings. Saul was no longer obeying God's commandments. When Saul left the cave, David screamed out to Saul and told him to look at the corner of his robe (1 Samuel 24:11). When Saul saw that he had lost a tassel and saw David holding it in his hands, he knew he was done for. His kingdom was over. Knowing this, Saul told David, *"And now, behold, I know that you shall surely be king, and that the kingdom of Israel shall be established in your hand"* (1 Samuel 24:20).

Saul knew that the image was that he lost the wing; he lost God's protection.

Now, as time went on, another prophecy came into play. In Malachi 4:2, God is speaking, and he says, *"But for you who fear my name, the sun of righteousness will rise with healing in its wings* (kanaph)*."* Sun of righteousness (*Shemesh tsedâqâh*) has been almost unanimously agreed upon by both Jewish and Christians alike to refer to the coming Messiah. *Shemesh* is the joining of two root words together: *shem* and *esh*. *Shem* has various meanings, like name, fame, and renown. And *esh* means fire, burning, or hot. Put together; it means the world-renown fire of righteousness has come with healings in his *kanaph*, his wings, his corner.[3]

This is also the last of the numerous Messianic prophesies in the Old Testament. After Malachi wraps up this chapter, there is a little over 400 years of total silence from God. There are no recordings that God spoke to anyone. God did not raise any more prophets to speak on his behalf. There were no angel sightings, prophecies, or anything from God for over 400 years. So for the Jews, this passage that the coming Messiah will have healing in his wings was significant. Add to that 400 years without God speaking to the people of Israel, and they longed for the coming Messiah to bring this healing.

Going back to the story, Jesus is walking, and he is in a hurry because a girl is sick and could die at any moment. The crowds are constrained all around him, and it's tough to walk without people bumping into him and Jesus banging into the people. It's a tense moment. During all that, another woman enters the scene, and she is sick and has been for a very long time. She went to all the physicians and nothing. She spent all her money on doctors and nothing. More than likely, she has come to terms with the fact that she will die because of this bleeding disorder.

On the brink of desperation, she hears that Jesus is in town. She has heard about his reputation. No doubt the echoing cries of those who encountered Jesus said he was the Messiah. And she thinks to herself, if he is the Messiah, he will surely come with healing in his wings. Doesn't the Bible say the Messiah, the son of righteousness, will come with healing in his wings? So, she comes up with a plan. If she can somehow anonymously get to where he is, and if she can touch the *"hem of his garment, "* she could be healed (Matthew 9:20 KJV). Hem is the Greek word, *kraspedon*, which is the Hebrew equivalent of *kanaph*, or corner.[4]

This woman believed the prophecy in Malachi and knew that if she could just touch one of the tassels on the corner of Jesus' robe, she would be healed. Now, I don't know about you, but I thought that if this woman had touched any part of Jesus' clothing, she thought she would be healed. No, she knew her Bible. She knew it had to be his tassels. She crept into the crowd, got close to Jesus, and grabbed the tassel with all her might hanging from his robe. And BOOM! Instantly she felt power enter her body, and she knew she was healed.

What does this tell you about Jesus? When was the last time you saw a picture of Jesus wearing tassels? I haven't seen one. Ever. Most of the pictures people have painted of Jesus have him with a halo hovering over his flowing long brown hair and wearing a pristine white robe. No tassels.

> *And behold, a woman…came up behind him and touched the fringe of his garment, for she said to herself, "if I only touch his garment, I will be made well"* (Matthew 9:20-21).

Why did this woman have such confidence that she would be made well? I mean, she went to every doctor known to man, and she was not made well. Why the change all of a sudden? This woman believed that Jesus was who he said he was. She believed that he was the Messiah and had come with healing in his wings.

THE GREAT DISTRACTION

> *And immediately the flow of blood dried up, and she felt in her body that she was healed of her disease* (Mark 5:29).

I am not sure I can imagine what this moment would have felt like for this woman. No doubt the pressing crowd seemed to cease moving. The world froze in a flash. Her bleeding stopped. A smile, maybe for the first time in twelve years, began to creep up on her face.

She was healed!

And Jesus, perceiving in himself that power had gone out from him, immediately turned about in the crowd and said, "Who touched my garments?" (Mark 5:30).

Not only is Jesus approachable and available, but he is also interruptible. Until this point, no words were said between this woman and Jesus. We know what she thought, but no one in the crowd knew, not even the disciples. She knew she was healed. Jesus knew she was healed. She could have just been thankful that this twelve-year illness was over with, and she could have slithered away in the same way she came. But Jesus wasn't done with this woman yet. In this moment of interruption, Jesus took charge of this woman's destiny and changed her life forever.

Here was this woman who was in need. She knew there was no answer or help coming on a physical level. She tried all she could to be healed and came up with no solution, only more sickness. She also knew she was a sinner. She lived with the symbol of sin (blood) every day of her life for the last twelve years. She had nothing. No money. No community. No family. No church. Nothing. The only thing she had left was to trust in the scriptures and have faith that Jesus was, in fact, the Messiah.

Jesus was looking for the person who touched him.

Silence.

"Who touched my garments?" (Mark 5:30).

Silence.

I can imagine at this point, Jesus is now looking at this woman. She knows he knows. Finally, she comes before him in fear and trembling and falls down and spills the beans.

"It was me! I touched you! And here is why...."

"Daughter, your faith has made you well; go in peace and be healed." (Mark. 5:34).

I don't know if you know this, but this is the only time in the Bible where Jesus calls any woman a daughter. Even though Jesus was interrupted, he took time to comfort this woman. He affirms to her that she can now go in peace, a word which Jesus doesn't use lightly. Anytime Jesus tells someone to go in peace, it refers to having a right relationship with God. This woman truly believed in the saving work of Jesus Christ.

From this interruption, this woman was brought back to health. She was returned to society. She was allowed to go back and embrace and kiss her family. She was now able to have fellowship with her church family. In the eyes of the people, she was now able to be restored back to God. What a beautiful moment this was for this woman.

Can you imagine what Jairus was thinking during this time? "Jesus, come on! We don't have time for interruptions!" As a matter of fact, after this interruption, word got out that Jairus' daughter had died. If I were Jairus, bitterness would have overrun my heart for this woman interrupting Jesus. If it were not for her, my daughter might still be alive! How dare you interrupt him!

Praise God, our savior, our hero, is unlike anyone on this planet! Jesus ends up going to Jairus' house and raising his daughter from death. Why? Because even though Jesus was interrupted, he is still available. I haven't forgotten about you, Jairus! Let's go! She is not dead; she is only taking a little nap—a happy ending for everyone involved.

I don't know about you, but I am filled with joy that my hero is not only approachable and available but he is also interruptible. Aren't you? But it should lead to another question: why don't we interrupt Jesus more? I mean, if we love the fact that our hero is willing to be interrupted, why don't we interrupt him more? Is it because we think our requests are too trivial to bother him? Is it because we are trying to protect ourselves from being disappointed if we do interrupt him? Do we feel as if what we want or need may be selfish or greedy, so there is no way Jesus will take time for me concerning this? Maybe we think our prayers, no matter how big or small, probably won't affect his sovereign plan, so why bother? Could it be that we would instead handle it ourselves most of the time than to interrupt Jesus? Are we relying on our strength instead of his? Haven't we learned by now that depending on our strength is exhausting and usually leaves us worse off than before? Or could it be that we never interrupt Jesus because we believe he is unwilling or unable to help us? Honestly, why don't we interrupt him more?

Have you not learned already that his love for you is irrational and that he relentlessly pursues you, even when you tend to wander? Haven't you learned that he runs towards you when you are still a long way off? Why in the world would we not go to him for everything! Come on, people! He doesn't mind being interrupted! He loves you too much to ignore you! You're his favorite!

How many times have you read in the New Testament where Jesus tells us to ask? *Whatever you ask in prayer, you will receive it, if you have faith* (Matthew 21:22). *Ask and it will be given to you* (Matthew 7:7). *Ask whatever you wish, and it will be done for you* (John 15:7). *Ask, and it will be given to you* (Luke 11:9). *Whatever you ask in prayer...it will be yours* (Mark 11:24). *Until now you have asked nothing in my name. Ask, and you will receive, that your joy may be full* (John 16:24). *If you ask for me anything in my name, I will do it* (John 14:14). *Whatever you ask the Father in my name, he may give it to you* (John 14:13). *How much more will the heavenly Father give you the Holy Spirit to those who ask him* (Luke 11:13). *Again I say to you, if two of you agree on earth about anything they ask, it will be done for them by my Father in heaven* (Matthew 18:19).

ASK! ASK! ASK!

INTERRUPT! INTERRUPT! INTERRUPT!

Jesus is always approachable.

Jesus is always available.

Jesus is always interruptible.

Jesus does not withhold from us. He is not stingy. He is consumed with love and affection for you! He is jealous of your fellowship, and he is personally present in your life—at every moment of your life. Trust me; he doesn't mind being interrupted by you. It doesn't matter how many issues are pressed against him. It doesn't matter how busy he is upholding the universe with the power of his word. He will stop in a moment to be with you! Do you believe that? Do you believe that our hero is available and interruptible? There is no one like Jesus. Don't ever forget that. What a hero we have!

Something to Think About...

1. In Mark 5:21-34, what are some similarities and differences between the woman and Jairus? What were some of the obstacles both had to overcome to reach out to Jesus for help?
2. In what ways do these two people, Jairus and the woman, most remind you of yourself?
3. Why do you think Jesus asked who touched him? What was the result of this question for the woman? For the crowd? For the disciples?
4. How can Jesus be available to you to grow your faith?
5. If Jesus is always interruptible, why don't we interrupt him more? What is it that is holding us back?

7

CHAPTER

Things Are Not What
They Appear

———◆———

MY SECOND WIFE...SORT OF

I was voted class clown and biggest flirt my senior year in high school. I graduated with only sixty-four kids in my class, so it was slim pickings when nominating people for stuff. I understood the class clown bit. I love to be silly and enjoy playing jokes on people. Ironically, I was about as shy as you could get when talking to girls I liked. Sure, if I knew I had no shot with someone, I would be my goofy, somewhat flirtatious self, but I clammed up when it came to asking out a girl! Things aren't always what they appear. Apparently, my classmates thought I was a flirt, which to them, it may have appeared that way, but they completely missed the mark on that. How I ended up being chosen for that was beyond my comprehension.

After I graduated high school, Jesus slammed into my soul and forever changed my life. I went to Kennesaw State University (close to Atlanta). I immediately got involved in Cru, where I met many great and beautiful people. Cru had a large conference in Atlanta during our Christmas break, and several of us from my school went. Schools from all over the Southeast attended. Prominent schools like the University of Alabama, Georgia, Auburn, Georgia Tech, and Florida were present. We met at a hotel in downtown Atlanta and spent three days listening to some great speakers and enjoying some break-out sessions on different topics. What I didn't know was that this impromptu trip to this conference would change my life forever.

When I first arrived, I was waiting to sign in when I saw this unbelievably beautiful woman about five people behind me in line. She was wearing blue jeans overalls (don't judge, they were in style back then) and a red turtleneck sweater. Her hair was in pigtails, and she looked marvelous! She was laughing with some friends, which drew my attention, and her smile was utterly intoxicating. I knew right then and there that I wanted to get to know this person. I mean, I was nominated as the biggest flirt, so it was a no-brainer that I could woo this woman off her feet.

For three days, I became a creepy little stalker. If I saw her go to a break-out session that talked about being missionaries to Sri Lanka, well, sign me up! I was going to Sri Lanka with her. If it were a session on basket weaving to reach the lost tribes in the dense Amazon rain forest, I would learn basket weaving to be with this woman. For three days, it went like this. If you were an outsider watching me, you would have felt great shame for my failed attempts to talk to her and probably frightened for this woman's safety!

Finally, as everything was wrapping up on the last day, I mustered enough courage to talk to her. I noticed this Greek statue-like handsome man, with his dumb perfect haircut and athletic genes talking to her, trying to get her email. I crept up to them, acting about as causal as a man getting a physical at the doctor's office, hoping to shoo this guy away from her. When I finally stood next to her, the handsome creature said, "Can I have your email?" We didn't have social media back then, so exchanging emails was preferred. She promptly gave it to him, and he hurried away. He probably saw my intimidating 135-pound frame and thought he better leave before I destroyed him! This was my moment. Three hard, grueling days of stalking have paid off with this brief moment in time.

She was looking at me.

I was looking at her.

Her gorgeous blue eyes were captivating and drew me in. Time stood still. Incidentally, so did my heart. Usually, when I got nervous, my heart would beat fast; now, it was like it stopped working altogether. That, of course, concerned me and made me take a huge breath right in front of her, making me look as if I were bored or impatient or were a goober who forgot how to breathe.

She was looking at me.

I was looking at her.

I also felt my tongue swell up, making my mouth go dry. What in the world was wrong with me? I CAN DO THIS, SCOTT! I am pretty sure if I don't say something now, I would not only blow my one shot, but she would probably think I was Mr. McCreepy staring at her like I was.

She was looking at me.

I was looking at her.

I took one more deep breath and went for it. For the first time since I met her, I finally dared to speak to this beautiful woman. I only said three words. Three magical words. Three powerful words. Three life-altering words. I said...

"Yeah, me too?" As I shoved my binder in her face.

Biggest flirt, whatever! Basically, I was playing off the conversation from the other dude and asked for her email. She was very gracious and wrote her name and email on the binder, and then she asked for mine. She handed me her binder, and I noticed the front page was covered entirely with around seventeen thousand other emails of dumb boys she met at the conference. That was a little disconcerting, but who cares. I felt like a Cheetah after a glorious kill! Regrettably, and for the life of me, I couldn't think of anything else to say, so I turned and left. Casanova would have been proud!

I got home, and my dad asked how the retreat went. Yes, I lived with my parents for most of my college years. Shut it!

"How did it go?"

"It was great! I learned how to basket weave."

"Money well spent."

"I know, right! Oh, and I also met my second wife."

"Say that again? Your what?"

I probably should clarify here. I was thoroughly convinced that I would marry the Russian tennis player Anna Kournikova. She was beautiful, athletic, and wealthy! Who wouldn't want her for a wife? Of course, language barriers would have been a problem at first, but I wasn't opposed to learning Russian. However, if things didn't work out with Anna, this woman at the Cru retreat would be my other wife.

Her name was Charlotte. She lived in Alabama, attending the University of Alabama. I kept that binder she wrote her name and email on for the rest of that semester. I constantly looked at her handwriting, thinking about what our lives could be like if we had a chance to start a relationship, barring Anna Kournikova turning me down, of course.

We were two kids living in two different states. How could this even work?

Now, I know what you are thinking. You are thinking about how long did it take me to email her. Did I do the customary two-day wait period, or did I blow it and impatiently email her as soon as I got home that evening? Well, first off, don't interrupt my story with irrelevant questions like that. And secondly, I—umm—didn't email her. I was too afraid! Honestly, I had no clue what to say. Where do you begin when it comes to the woman of your dreams? I guess you could say I had writer's block, but more than likely, I was just being my dumb old self, shutting down, and being all shy and senseless when it came to girls I liked.

Miracles of miracles! She was the one to email first! About a month later, I got the first email. It took a month because she probably wondered what in the world was taking me so long. Or she was emailing those other seventeen thousand guys she met at the conference and realized they were just no-good lousy pieces of dirt with fantastic hair underserving of her time and attention. So, let's email that stalker from the Cru retreat! I have no clue. She never said, and I never asked. I was just thankful she took the first step and reached out to this big flirt.

We both attended the Cru retreat again at Christmas break and were inseparable the following year. The last night we stayed up in the hotel lobby talking and getting to know each other better. As we talked, she found out I was heading for full-time ministry and liked to play the guitar. I found out she was a vegetarian, and I almost broke it off with her right then. Boy, what a disappointment that piece of news was! She eats fish and eggs, so she is not an actual vegetarian, but it becomes too long and too difficult to pronounce the way she says it—something like an ovo-lacto-pesco-something-or-other. Talk about things are not what they appear. Here is this perfect woman, and she claims she doesn't eat chicken or beef? Not only that but what do you say to that. I put on a cheesy smile and said, "Oh! That's cool!" It was one of the many lies I have spoken in my life!

Thankfully, her other qualities overcame that colossal hurdle in our relationship! I would later find out that she was praying for a godly man to come her way. I let her know that Anna Kournikova had yet to answer my calls, so I guess she was it!

We dated for about a year and a half, and by the grace of God, we got married! Our honeymoon night was at the same hotel in Atlanta where we first met. It was beautiful and romantic and everything you could ever dream of. Who knew that when I told my dad that I met my wife, she would become my wife one day? Those three words, "Yeah, me too?" must have sealed the deal on this one! I'm so smooth!

Do you know what honeymoon means? It means a sweet month. That's it. A month! Maybe it will last two months, perhaps a little longer if we are lucky. Eventually, the honeymoon stage ends, and reality kicks in. My wife, bless her heart, decided early on in our relationship to put me on a pedestal. When reality kicked her in the face, she may have been thinking about buyer's remorse! She thought she was getting everything she prayed to God for; an outrageously good-looking man (jokes on her!), a godly man who loves Jesus, and an extroverted conversationalist. I was far from all of that. At the time, I was a skinny, awkward guy who tried to be godly but sinned often. I loved Jesus with all my heart, yet I was often prone to wander.

To make matters worse, I am not extroverted like my wife; I'm introverted. I do not have the conversational dexterity my wife has, nor all the words she can use in each twenty-four-hour period. Plus, I turn into a troll after nine o'clock. How she has stayed with me for so long is a miracle. All I know is that she was probably hoping when she married me that she was getting a fillet mignon but ended with a flounder instead. She is a vegetarian, so maybe she prayed for flounder and got fillet mignon instead. Who knows, but I am sure when she married me, she realized fast that things were not what they appeared.

THINGS ARE NOT WHAT THEY APPEAR

I want to point out a story that Jesus shared about two completely different people, and as we go through it, we will realize that things are not what they appear in this story. In Luke 18, Jesus will blow away the minds of all who

He also told this parable to some who trusted in themselves that they were righteous and treated others with contempt: "Two men went up into the temple to pray, one a Pharisee and the other a tax collector. The Pharisee, standing by himself, prayed thus: 'God, I thank you that I am not like other men, extortioners, unjust, adulterers, or even like this tax collector. I fast twice a week; I give tithes of all that I get.' But the tax collector, standing far off, would not even lift up his eyes to heaven, but beat his breast, saying, 'God, be merciful to me, a sinner!' I tell you, this man went down to his house justified, rather than the other. For everyone who exalts himself will be humbled, but the one who humbles himself will be exalted. (Luke 18:9-14)

This is a fascinating story, one in which Jesus is demonstrating that things are not what they appear. In Jesus' time, the dominant religious idea, and honestly, the prevailing religious belief today, is the notion that good people should go to heaven. In other words, if you are morally good, you can have salvation and become right in the eyes of God. It's all just a matter of how morally or spiritually good you are. Simply put, you can earn heaven by just being a good guy or a good girl.

"He also told this parable to some who trusted in themselves that they were righteous" (Luke 18:9). People, throughout time, have bought into this idea that I can earn heaven by being good, and trusting in my morality, my religious behaviors, or actions. The Pharisee in this story was the most intensely, careful, law-keeping, and moral person on the planet. He has spent his entire life lining himself up with God's law. He doesn't partake in all the other pagan festivities. He is all about the Bible and what God has to say. This guy is about as good as you can get.

On the other hand, the tax collector was about as bad as one can get. He was a self-confessed sinner and the most despised of all outcasts. Yet, the tax collector went home justified and not the good old boy! Something is not what it appears.

If the good boy is out and the bad boy is in, we probably need to better understand God's requirement of "good." In Leviticus 20:26, God says, *"You shall be holy to me, for I the LORD am holy and have separated you from the peoples, that you should be mine."* Essentially God is saying if you want to know what my standards of good are, then just be absolutely holy.

Pause.

How are we doing with that? Are you always holy? God knows I am not. Yeah, God, your standard seems to be slightly high here. No one can meet this standard.

Okay, forget God, let's go to my hero Jesus and see what he has to say. *"You therefore must be perfect as your heavenly Father is perfect"* (Matt 5:48). Ugh! Is anyone perfect? Yeah, probably not even close.

This Pharisee is about as near as you can be to being holy and perfect, yet he's not even close. You must be as good as God, or as holy as God, or as perfect as Jesus. James will add salt to the wound by saying, *"For whoever keeps the whole law but fails in one point has become guilty of all of it"* (James 2:10). That's a bummer! I guess there is no way to get to God based on our morality, law-keeping, or religious efforts. We are a long way off from being perfect.

Luke 18:10: *"Two men went up to the temple to pray, one a Pharisee and the other a tax collector."* Twice a day, people in Jerusalem would go to the temple to pray. The word "pray" here is just another way of saying worshiping God. Those two times were at nine o'clock in the morning and three in the afternoon. Those were when the priests held the morning and evening sacrifices in the temple. Numbers 28 explicitly details this. No need to go into all the particulars, but there were sin offerings, which were sacrifices that would atone the Jewish people of their sins. There was a priestly blessing, an offering of incense which symbolized the prayers offered to God, a lamb was sacrificed, and other things were going on during these daily sacrifices.[1]

Twice, every single day.

Without fail.

During one of those sacrifices, a Pharisee and tax collector walked into the temple to pray and worship God. Talk about polar opposites. The Pharisee is the most religious man in the world. In all respect, they were the most esteemed and honored of all Jewish men during that time. The tax collector could easily be seen as the most despised person. They were despised because they purchased tax franchises from the Romans. Romans were the ones who conquered all of Israel and were occupying their land. Jews longed for the day that God would wipe them out from the face of the earth. There was no love there when it came to the Romans. The tax collectors were taxing the Jewish people to fund the Roman army, which the Jewish people so desperately wanted out of their land. They would then take the tax money and give the Romans what the agreed-upon tax was for that year, and anything they had leftover, they kept for themselves. Most tax collectors would add extra fees or inflate the tax so they could make tons of money. They were extortionists, basically.

Luke 18:11-12: *"The Pharisee, standing by himself, prayed thus: 'God, I thank you that I am not like other men, extortioners, unjust, adulterers, or even like this tax collector. I fast twice a week. I give tithes of all that I get.'"* Let's be honest; this Pharisee was praying to himself; he just used the title "God" because that was the honorable thing to do, especially in the temple during the sacrifice. Nevertheless, it was all about himself. Have you ever prayed to yourself? Probably not because you would sound like a lunatic.

"Dear Scott, I just want to thank you for how awesome you really are! And your beautiful wife is pretty lucky to have a guy like you!"

"Oh, Great Scott, thank you for your coolness and adorable outlook on life!"

"Dear Mighty Scott, keep living your dream of being the biggest flirt and class clown! Because of your greatness, you deserve nothing but the best!"

This Pharisee doesn't have much of a relationship with God at all. By his prayer, he doesn't have much connection with God either. This prayer is nothing more than a self-induced monolog of his moral goodness. Five times in two verses, he uses the word "I." It's all about me, myself, and I. Sure, he will implore the name of God but come on, that is just a reputable thing to do, but he asks God for downright nothing. Why? There is nothing to ask God in his view because he cannot think of anything that he needs from him. I am just going to stand off by myself, with my chest held high, and do a little inventory of my life. Yep, I knew it! I am awesome! I lack nothing. How cool am I?

Why would this Pharisee thank God? In his eyes, he was the one who achieved everything. WOW! I am so good! I am not like these other scum standing in the temple. I am not like those adulterers over there or that unjust vermin standing there. Wait! Who is that? Oh, dear God, I am so blessed. I am not like that tax collector standing in the corner! What a despicable disgrace. How disgusting is he! Nope, I am better than that. I fast twice a week. Side note here—did you know that God only required his people to fast just once a year? During the Day of Atonement, God commanded all his people to fast and pray. Just once a year. But not me, God! I am too cool for school. I am too holy for my guacamole. I will fast twice a week. And speaking of awesome, I also tithe everything I get. Yeah, can anyone top that? Anyone? I didn't think so. Look how good I am!

This Pharisee totally ignored what God said in the book of Amos. In Amos chapter four, God talks about Israel being taken into captivity because these people have forsaken him and are doing whatever their hearts desire. They think they are good, but it is not what it appears. In response to this, God will go all sarcastic on these people. *"Come to Bethel, and transgress; to Gilgal, and multiply transgressions; bring your sacrifices every morning, your tithes every three days; offer a sacrifice of thanksgiving of that which is leavened, and proclaim freewill offerings, publish them; for so you love to do, O people of Israel!"* (Amos 4:4-5). In case you are wondering, that is God being sarcastic. It is sarcasm born from self-righteous people who have bought into warped self-righteous religion of their own making. It is sarcasm based on the notion that people think they can earn righteousness by being good. This Pharisee is just like the people of old. Man, I am so good! I am so moral. I am so religious. Thank goodness I am so much better than everybody else. God must really love me.

Luke 18:13: *"But the tax collector, standing far off, would not even lift up his eyes to the heaven, but beat his breast, saying, 'God, be merciful to me, a sinner!'"* Jesus shifts gears, and now we get to see the realities that Jesus wants us to understand. Tax collectors are loathed and the most defiled of all people. They are loathed because they take my money! They are defiled because they constantly handle the money of the Romans, and on each coin is a graven image of Caesar himself. Most of the Caesars claimed to be god-like, so just by touching those coins, you are defiling the commands of God because they have graven images of people posing as gods. It was why tax collectors were not allowed to enter the local synagogues. Incidentally, they were seen as the farthest away spiritually from God. Jesus is giving us an excellent contrast of people. He gives us the most righteous person he can think of and the most despicable person.

The Pharisee is probably standing in the temple as close to the altar, or the Holy of Holies, as he can get. This guy believes he belongs there! Plus, everyone can see him standing so close to God's inner sanctum, which is where he wants everyone to see him worshiping. The tax collector, by contrast, is standing the farthest away as he can get. More than likely at the corner of the temple where he can still be a part of the worship, but not close to the others who are more righteous than him. He knows he doesn't deserve to be in the presence of God. He also knows he doesn't even deserve to be in the company of God's people. Look at all these righteous people. Who am I among these saints! I am nothing but a sinner. And he knows it. Not only am I a pariah to society, but I am a pariah to God. He feels like he is alienated from God, as seen by his location in the temple.

I am a nobody!

Even his posture would suggest that. He couldn't even lift his eyes to heaven. Back then, worshipers would have their eyes lifted toward the heavens and their hands raised when they worshiped in the temple. It was a way of showing whom you are worshiping and lifting the hands to say I surrender to whatever God gives, whether it be his grace, forgiveness or mercy. This man couldn't even look up. He was overwhelmed with guilt and shame. He knows he is unworthy. He knows it. He feels it. He believes it. He even confesses it. There is no attitude here. There is no self-righteous behavior going on in this man. This tax collector could have said, "Well, at least I am here at church. I don't see all my other tax-collecting buddies here. They don't even go to church!" No, he feels the total weight of his estrangement from God.

With his eyes down, he starts to beat his chest. Repeatedly. It is a gesture that expresses the most extreme sorrow and anguish. With it came conviction and remorse. He is truly feeling the weight of his sin and brokenness.

This beating of the chest was seen when Christ was crucified. Luke 23:48 says, *"And all the crowds that had assembled for this spectacle, when they saw what had taken place, returned home beating their breasts."* The horrific event of Jesus' death was an occurrence of profound anguish, and the men and women who saw it reacted by beating their chests. Here, the tax collector feels this same type of pain, brokenness, and sorrow. Here in the temple, in the presence of God, he is crushed and humbled.

"God, be merciful to me, a sinner!" (Luke 18:13). In the original Greek language, there is a definitive article here. It translates, "Have mercy on me, THE sinner!" This tax collector thinks he is the worst sinner out there. Of all the people that he knows, and of all the other tax collectors that he knows, he has deemed himself the worst of them all. As far as his knowledge of other people is concerned, he is the nastiest, vilest, and worst of the lot.

Being merciful to me means to propitiate. It means to appease or to make satisfaction. This guy says, "God, please apply the atonement to me!" God, please cover me with the atonement made during this sacrifice. Atonement is a big churchy word that just means to cover over.[2] This guy understood the scriptures and why these sacrifices happened every day at nine and three, and that the sacrifices were a symbolic to the fact that God would appease people's sins by sacrifice. This man is saying that he is a wretched sinner. He is unworthy to stand near the presence of God and he is in profound agony and anguish over his sins. He is also very aware that he needs atonement to apply those sins to him. Please, God, let this sacrifice, this picture of your atonement, cover me! Please, God, let it be applied to me!

Jesus takes two polar opposites, and he pits them against each other. If we think about it, though, these two did have a lot in common. They both would agree that the Bible was the revelation of God. They both believe that the God of the Old Testament was the creator God. They both believe God was a God of mercy and compassion. They also believe that God was a God of righteousness, holiness, and even justice. Undoubtedly, both believe that God was a God of forgiveness. They believed in the same God, the same Scriptures, and the same theological notion that God can atone for sins. They were not far apart theologically.

The only difference was that one repented, and the other didn't think he needed to repent. One knew he was wrong and guilty; the other didn't think he ever did anything wrong.

Jesus says in Luke 18:14, *"I tell you; this man went down to his house justified, rather than the other. For everyone who exalts himself will be humbled, but the one who humbles himself will be exalted."*

Things are not what they appear.

Can you imagine the crowd's reaction to what Jesus just said? What? How can this be? The tax collector was justified and not the Pharisee? How in the world can this man be justified? He is a tax collector, for goodness sakes! Jesus, have you lost your mind!

Justified means to be made right. More to the point, it means to be made righteous in the eyes of God. How can this be? For Jesus, he says that the only righteousness that God will accept is perfect righteousness. Since you and I cannot earn that, God will give it freely as a gift to those who repent and trust him.

This tax collector didn't do anything to be right in the eyes of God. His life, response, and posture clearly showed that he did not deserve God's mercy. He just stood there hoping, praying, and wishing that God would have mercy on him, a sinner. And that right there is all it took for Jesus to notice and cover him with his love and forgiveness. All he did was just receive the gift that God gave him. The Pharisee, on the other hand, left in his self-righteousness, never being covered by Christ. His pride only intensified his alienation from God. Atonement is worthless to the self-righteous.

> **JESUS IS MY HERO BECAUSE NO MATTER WHAT I HAVE DONE OR WILL DO, JESUS WILL TAKE THE WRAP AND COVER FOR ME**

THE COURTROOM OF GOD

Have you ever had a friend who would go to prison for you? Those are the friends you want to keep for life. You are like, "Hold my beer—umm—I mean water!" They are the first to grab it as you do some wild, foolish thing. They are always there for you, even when you do something outrageously ill-advised. You are thick as thieves, and there is no one better to have in your corner than that person because you know they will always have your back. Better yet, they would be willing to take the rap for you if things go horrifically wrong. Jesus is my hero because he is that type of friend. He has no problem taking the rap for the dumb things I do. He has no problem covering up my ill-advised transgressions. Indeed, he is some kind of friend.

The apostle John says in 1 John 2:1, *"My little children, I am writing these things to you so that you may not sin. But if anyone does sin, we have an advocate with the Father, Jesus Christ the righteous."* John teaches us a compelling lesson here about how things don't always seem as they appear. For example, God is a God of justice, which means every dumb, sinful thing we do, needs to be punished. Proverbs 11:21 says, *"Be assured, an evil person will not go unpunished."* Nahum 1:3 adds, *"The LORD is slow to anger and great in power, and the LORD will by no means clear the guilty."* Scripture is unequivocal that every sin will be punished. One of the most brutal truths of the Bible is that every sin ever committed by anyone, at any time, known or unknown, will not go unpunished. God's mercy will not deteriorate his determination for justice to be absolute.

John could have said, "If anyone sins—haha—you will pay! Fools!" We would probably not like it, but we would understand. We all know we are sinners. However, that wouldn't make Jesus much of a hero at all. He would be seen as more of the villain in this story as he seeks vengeance on those who have done him wrong. What makes Jesus a hero is that every single sin that we have ever committed will demand punishment, but the sinner who puts their trust in Jesus will be granted mercy instead. That right there is how the tax collector received mercy and not justice.

Let's go to the courtroom of God and see how this plays out. First, let's look at the indictment: *"If anyone does sin"* (1 John 2:2). Real quick, have you ever sinned? Yeah, me too. So, we are sinners, and we are in the courtroom guilty. God has a complete record of all our wrongs to add insult to injury.

Additionally, as Christians, we strive to have holy ambitions, be more diligent in obeying God's word, and endeavor to be morally good people, but we still sin. All the time. The indictment is clear. The Judge knows we are guilty. We know we are guilty. And amazingly, our advocate, our defense lawyer, knows we are guilty.

What is more, the prosecutor knows we are guilty as well. And this prosecutor is eager to push this case before the Judge and demand that God be true to his justice and punish us for our crime. Of course, the prosecutor is Satan himself.

Look at Revelation 12:10. *"And I heard a loud voice in heaven, saying, 'Now the salvation and the power and the kingdom of our God and the authority of his Christ have come, for the accuser of our brothers has been thrown down, who accuses them day and night before our God.'"* This accuser, the prosecutor, has been going before God day and night, accusing us of all our wrongdoings before God. I mean, he is at the throne of God day and night, bringing accusations against us. And he will continue to do so until that verse is fulfilled when Christ comes back. Obviously, the second coming of Christ hasn't happened yet, so Satan is constantly in God's ear trying to condemn us for all the sins we have committed. He is ruthless. He is a hateful prosecutor who cries out to God relentlessly to force God's hand of justice and render the punishment that should rightly be given to us. Let's just say he is not in favor of mercy. He hates mercy.

So, we are in the courtroom. The indictment is clear, and everyone knows we are guilty. We look up, and in walks the Judge. I don't know about you, but I may be wetting my pants right about now because the Judge happens to be God himself, who knows everything I have ever done in great detail.

Unfortunately, this is not a jury trial.

The Judge is formidable and doesn't need a jury of peers to come up with a verdict. He doesn't need others to help him interpret the law; he was the one who wrote it! So, if we are going to be cleared of all our wrongdoing, this Judge, who wrote the law on wrongdoing, will have to free us.

It's not looking so good.

If I had to go before a holy God who would judge me for all my offenses, I would probably want the best defense attorney money could buy. Thankfully, we have the best one in the world. As a matter of fact, our defense attorney has never lost a case. Not only that, but the Judge— well—the Judge is his father. And get this: the Judge personally appointed us this defense attorney.

Listen again to what John said. *"But if anyone does sin, we have an advocate with the Father, Jesus Christ the righteous. He is the propitiation for our sins, and not for ours only but also for the sins of the whole world"* (1 John 2:1-2). Propitiation is the exact same thing as atonement. As I mentioned before, it means appeasing, bringing satisfaction, or covering over. Jesus is the best defense attorney you and I can ever have because he is the only one that can claim that he paid the price for whatever wrongdoing you and I have ever committed. The death of Christ on the cross was not just a random event in the flow of history; it was an earth-shattering announcement to Satan and the rest of the world that God will be a God of justice by placing all the world's sin on Jesus' shoulders. All sin will be punished, and that punishment fell on Jesus to take, which means Jesus is the only one who can take the rap for us and cover our sins. Thus, the justice of God is satisfied, appeased by Christ, and the mercy of God is granted to us.

So, if we sin? Well, the prosecutor will jump up from his seat and yell out to the Judge. The prosecutor demands that we deserve justice and for the Judge to throw the book at us. He wants all of us punished! But our advocate, our defense attorney, our hero, has proven that he has already covered that.

I know what you are thinking. You are thinking that I said I would not talk about Jesus dying for our sins? You are correct. But understand this goes deeper than Jesus being our savior and dying on the cross. Jesus takes a step further where not only has he died for our sins, but he will constantly be advocating on our behalf every time we forget the great sacrifice he made for us when we continue to keep on sinning. He is more than just a savior to us; he should be our best friend. He's got our back. Always! He will take the rap and go to jail for you!

You know, the longer I am a follower of Jesus, do you know what I tend to do? I tend to become numb to this idea that Jesus constantly takes the rap and covers for me. Do you know what I mean? If I sin, I am usually like, "Ah—my bad! —Sorry, Jesus!" And then I move on as if nothing happened at all. I sin again, oops! Sorry, buddy!

How often do we think about the fact that Jesus, right now, is in the courtroom of God battling it out with Satan, taking the rap for what you have done and is covering for you? How often are we reminded that Satan is categorically relentless, going to God day and night and trying to get him to condemn us to hell? He wants nothing more than to lock us up and throw away the key. Don't go numb to this! More than anything, don't ever forget that we have a hero who is not afraid to stand toe to toe with Satan because he is ever more relentless in his love for us than Satan is in his hate.

I've never really met anyone like Jesus. I have never met anyone who loves me as he does. I know my wife loves me, but I am confident she's glad we got married after the Flood in Noah's day. Before the flood, people lived to be around 800 years of age. Nowadays, you can be happily married for around 40 to 50 years. Back then—700! My wife would kill me around our 120th anniversary. Charlotte means the world to me, but even she won't take the rap and cover for me if I do something outlandishly sinful or unlawful. My best friends may take a bullet for me, but I am pretty sure they wouldn't go to jail for me or take the rap for something I did. But Jesus?

All the time.

Every time.

You cannot quantify his love. His love is too deep, too wide, and too irrational. Every day and every night, he advocates on my behalf and takes the rap for something he didn't do. Why he continues to cover for me is a mystery. I will never have the answer, but he will forever be my hero because of it.

Something to Think About...

1. In Jesus' time and even in ours, the dominant religious idea is that good people should go to heaven. What does Jesus say to this notion in Luke 18:9-14?
2. Why do most Christians believe that if I am just a good person, then indeed God loves me? Have you ever thought that? What do you think now?
3. How do we define good? How do you think Jesus defines good?
4. How often do we picture Jesus in heaven advocating on our behalf in front of God and Satan?
5. Why is it easier for us to exalt ourselves than being humble?

8

CHAPTER

Is it Ready Now?

<hr>

THE WORST WEDDING EVER

I remember the first wedding I ever officiated. It was a Friday, and my best friend and I planned a fishing trip. The day was a little overcast, and all our gear and poles were packed. We were ready to hit the water to catch as many slimy little creatures as we could as my friend and I embellished stories about our student ministries. We were both student pastors at the time, and we could embellish stories like the best of them. As a matter of fact, I believe you will never be a good pastor if you don't know how to embellish stories. Oh, sure, some may call that fibbing on things that are not factually correct. Some may even call it a white lie. I like to call it art.

By rule, every time we fished together, we played a game where the loser had to pay for lunch. The game entailed whoever caught the first fish, the largest fish, and the most fish, and the one who carried two out of the three would win. He beat me last time, so I planned on hooking the fish early to get a free lunch.

We were about an hour into the trip when my cell phone rang. It was one of my students. Everything in me was screaming, don't answer the phone. I was up three fish to one, and I didn't want to get distracted. But my friend was like, you better answer that.

"Hello."

"Scott?"

"Yeah, what's up, John?"

"Hey, so I need to ask you for a favor. A big one."

"Sure man, whatcha need? I am with my buddy fishing right now, so if you need me immediately, I am not sure I can be there in time."

"No, I don't need you right now, but I need you tonight."

"No worries, I can be there. What's up?"

"Well, my sister is getting married tonight, and the preacher who was going to do it bailed on her, and now we have no one to do the wedding. Can you do it?"

"You're telling me that the pastor bailed on your sister's wedding on the day of her wedding?"

"Yeah."

"That's not good!"

"Tell me about it. She is worried and stressed right now!"

"I bet. Alright, look, when is the wedding supposed to be?"

"Six o'clock"

"Okay, I will be there at five to meet with your sister and her future husband, and then we will have the wedding at six."

"Oh my goodness, Scott, you are God's greatest gift to mankind! I will name my first child after you!"

Okay, I embellished that last bit.

I'm sitting in that fishing boat, and my mind is spinning. First off, what kind of no-good pastor would bail on the wedding day of a marriage that they committed to officiating in the first place? Secondly, I had never done a wedding before, so all I was thinking about was getting back home and going over what I will say and how I will say it. Not only did we cut our trip short, but I had to pay for his lunch again. Double whammy! You guessed it, my mind was no longer into fishing, and I lost again.

I called my wife on the way home and told her the news. "Babe! I am doing a wedding tonight, and I want you there! It's my first one! It's going to be a great evening!" In hindsight, I wish I had never invited her. In hindsight, I wish I never agreed to do it. In hindsight, I should have kept fishing because the place I took my buddy for his free lunch made my stomach hurt.

I got directions to their house and turned into their gravel driveway at five o'clock. It took me into the middle of the woods, in the middle of Nowhere, Georgia, for about half a mile. Have you ever seen those horror movies where teenage kids would go to a deserted house in the middle of nowhere, only to be brutally murdered by some vile evil monster? Well, it wasn't like that, but it was close. Dead cars were all over the side of the road as if it was a warning to take myself and my car and get out of there. I persevered, though, and made it over a ridge where I saw a double-wide trailer. I assumed this was the place. Trash and what looked like every appliance known to man were scattered and broken all over the yard. As I parked, a young lady was smoking a cigarette on what I guess was their front porch. I hopped out and was going to introduce myself.

She threw the cigarette down and smashed it with the heel of her flip flop, stood up, and started walking towards me. I noticed she was about eight months pregnant!

"You the preacher?"

"Maybe."

"I'm the one getting married!"

She looked maybe eighteen, and at this point, I was seriously reconsidering what I was doing here. I forgive you, preacher man, whoever you are, that bailed on this couple!

"Is your groom here so we can all meet?"

"Yeah, he is in the back playing video games."

Of course, he is.

I walked in, and she directed me to the back bedroom. Several people were in the house, and all of them were looking at me, but no one said anything. Awkward. The groom looked fifteen years of age. He must have been in a very intriguing game on the Xbox because he didn't even want to talk when I came in. I finally made him turn it off and look at me. When they settled down, we talked a bit about how they met and what their plans were for the future, especially their baby's future. The boy had no job and dropped out of high school. The girl, also jobless, was about to have the baby in about a month. After listening to their story, I said something I had never spoken before or since to a soon-to-be-married couple. I said, "Are you sure you want to get married? I mean, really, really sure? We don't have to do this." The bride piped up, "YES, WE DO! We are in love!"

I finally met the bride's dad and found out the house we were in was his, and the wedding would be done in the living room. At this point, I was itching to get this over with, so I could go home and never speak of this to anyone. Eventually, we all were getting in position when my wife walked in the house, dressed in a beautiful, full-length dress as she was expecting an elegant wedding. Her hair was masterfully done with the right number of curls. The makeup was flawless. She looked beautiful. She looked like she was going to attend a wedding at a palace and not in the living room of a double-wide trailer. If I weren't so mortified at what was going down, I would have laughed out loud at the look on my wife's face when she saw how this was playing out. The dad and mom of the bride were in blue jeans and t-shirts. I never met the parents of the groom. A couple of cousins finished out this majestic ensemble. The living room was a mess, and I kid you not, two shotguns were lying on the end table. I would have paid money to know the thoughts flowing through Charlotte's mind when she took it all in.

As I was going through the declaration of intention during the wedding ceremony, someone walked in the front door (which opened into the living room), saw what was going on, cussed, and then walked out. The dad grunted something unintelligent, and I could swear my wife hadn't even blinked yet! Finally, we got to the exchanging of vows, and as the groom and bride were holding hands, the bride's dad shouted out, "BABY! You don't have to marry this guy!"

Oh, no! It's about to go down!

The look this girl gave her dad will haunt me forever. "Dad, I love him," she snarled more than she said. Dear Lord, I thought there would be a bloodbath, and no one was going to walk away alive. We were so far out in the woods I am sure it would take years for anyone to notice our decomposing bodies. My wife kept looking between the dad and the front door, knowing that if he made a move towards those shotguns, she would bolt, leaving me to my demise. I wouldn't have blamed her; I would have done the same if my wife had brought me to this debacle.

"Do you?"

"I Do!"

"Do You?"

"Yeah."

"Good enough for me. See ya!"

I have never left a place faster than I did that day. The taillights of Charlotte's car made their way down the driveway before I even got to my car. We both sat on our couch for about an hour without saying anything. Both of us were lost in thought of what we had just witnessed and were a part of. Finally, I looked at her and said, "If you tell anyone about this, I will deny it, and then I will disown you!"

A BETTER WEDDING

Thinking about Jesus as our hero cannot be complete if we don't discuss the wedding at Cana. This wedding was the polar opposite of the one I just described. This wedding was a feast and celebration of all God has brought together. Family and friends were present, filled with laughter and joy that only a consensual wedding can bring.

Cana was a small town about nine miles from Nazareth, where Jesus grew up. People from Nazareth would know people in Cana, and more than likely several were probably related. They assumedly farmed together and traded together. People were not as mobile as we are today. With Mary's family living in Nazareth for generations, more than likely, she knew many of the people in Cana. As we will see, she knew the people at the wedding very well.

Let me share a little about marriage here. The fact that Jesus did his first miracle at a wedding emphasizes the sanctity of this special covenant. Peter calls marriage the *"grace of life"* (1 Peter 3:7). Marriage is the most wonderful and blessed of all common graces God gives to us. By "common grace," I mean God pours out his grace to all people without any concern about whether they believe in him or not—that is common grace. We can see God's common grace when we look at a beautiful sunset, have a healthy long life, enjoy a great meal, or even fall in love. However, the height of all common graces is marriage. It is the best gift God can give us without any regard to whether we believe in him or not.

This means if any culture honors the sacredness of marriage, or if any society elevates the lifelong commitment of marriage, then that culture will be blessed by God. It will be a prosperous and safe place that experiences a degree of peace and security. At least historically. But suppose a society fails to honor marriage, belittles marriage, or distorts it. In that case, there will be disorder and chaos in that culture. I say that because where marriage for life is not honored, where the covenant between a husband and wife is not kept, then immorality will abound. It always does. We have seen this throughout the corridors of history. Anytime you go somewhere where sin is in control, it will overrun any culture or society. Marriage then, is a sacred and beautiful thing that should never be taken lightly or flippantly.

Okay, my marriage rant is over.

Let's look at this wedding in Cana.

> On the third day there was a wedding at Cana in Galilee, and the mother of Jesus was there. Jesus also was invited to the wedding with his disciples. When the wine ran out, the mother of Jesus said to him, "They have no wine." And Jesus said to her, "Woman, what does this have to do with me? My hour has not yet come." His mother said to the servants, "Do whatever he tells you." Now there were six stone water jars there for the Jewish rites of purification, each holding twenty or thirty gallons. 7 Jesus said to the servants, "Fill the jars with water." And they filled them up to the brim. And he said to them, "Now draw some out and take it to the master of the feast." So they took it. When the master of the feast tasted the water now become wine and did not know where it came from (though the servants who had drawn the water knew), the master of the feast called the bridegroom and said to him, "Everyone serves the good wine first, and when people have drunk freely, then the poor wine. But you have kept the good wine until now." This, the first of his signs, Jesus did at Cana in Galilee, and manifested his glory. And his disciples believed in him. (John 2:1-11)

During ancient times, you had arranged marriages. Personally, I like that. I have a daughter, and I would love to pick out her husband for her. Yeah, I know, that is frowned upon in our culture, but what's a dad to do! In an arranged marriage in the ancient Jewish culture, first, you had two dads get together and determine the likelihood that their kids are getting together. If both agreed, the groom's dad would pay the price for his son to marry the other dad's daughter. He would offer maybe several gallons of virgin olive oil or maybe two dozen sheep and a camel.

When my wife and I visited Israel, we were about to walk into one of the gardens at the Garden of Gethsemane, where an older Jewish gentleman stood by the gate. He looked at Charlotte, then at me, and then at Charlotte again. He finally looked back at me, and I kid you not, with complete soberness, he said, "I will give you a thousand camels for her," as he pointed to my wife. I was shocked! Did this guy just offer to buy my wife? I mean, my wife is drop-dead gorgeous, but that was extremely crude, no matter what culture you are in. But more importantly, how much do camels sell for nowadays? I am not good at math, and because I could not come up with the price a thousand camels would get me right then in my head, I told him, "Sorry, buddy, she is all mine." Who knows, I could have been rich! Dumb math!

If the dads agree upon a price, the dads will get the bride and groom together, and they would write out a covenant, and then the groom-to-be would offer a cup of wine to the bride.[1] If the bride refused, which rarely happened because it would disgrace her father, the wedding was off. But if she takes the cup of wine, it would be as if she was saying, "I will offer my life to you. I will be your one and only and live to serve you and you alone. I will love you for the rest of my life." She would then hand it back to the groom, and he would take a drink which would signify his undying love for this girl. At this point, the betrothal period would begin. Betrothal was a little more intense than our engagements today. Betrothals meant you were officially married, even though you hadn't consecrated the marriage. If you wanted to get out of the wedding, you had to file for a divorce certificate, even though you never slept together.

The bride would then spend the remaining time until the groom came for her, preparing to be a wife. She would learn the art of cooking, sewing, mending, and other needed tasks of that time. The groom would go back to his father's house, and he was required to build an addition to the house where his family lived. He had to make it himself. As you can imagine, this can take a while. He would have to lay out the foundation, work the angles, cut the stones and build a small one or two-room house adjacent to his parent's place. This would likely take around a year to complete because they had other duties and chores.

The dad would oversee the work to ensure he got it all right. This dad has been here before, so he knows the whole house could come crashing down on them if not done correctly. Plus, he knew the boy was probably thinking of only the honeymoon and how he wished it could come quicker, so he would watch the son build, lest he may skimp on some areas.

"You need to work on that angle over there. It doesn't look right."

"No! The window is too big!"

"Really! Son, where is the door supposed to be!"

"You're not ready."

As it was near completion, I can imagine the son going to his father constantly saying, "Is it ready now?" Which is to say, "Can I get my bride now?"

"It is ready now, dad?"

"Not yet. It is not time yet."

"But when?"

"When it's ready?"

"Is it ready now?"

Anticipation is such a beautiful and frustrating thing. But when it was time, let the party begin! When the dad deemed the house was ready, the boy and his family would head to the bride's house, and when they drew near, they would blow the shofar (a ram's horn) to announce that the groom had come. The bride and her entire party would head to the groom's house that he had just built, and they would have the wedding. The wedding in that culture would last around seven days. The tradition of ancient Jewish weddings is quite beautiful. I would have loved to experience one of them!

JESUS FINALLY STEPPING OUT

After thirty years of obscurity, Jesus is finally stepping out into the world. After thirty years of living a private life, he is now about to begin his public ministry. The bridge between the two is a wedding with friends and family. There is something cool about that. You would have thought that his first miracle would have been in Jerusalem or in front of some high-powered religious elites. Nope, it was in the small village of Cana with friends and family. By the way, Joseph is not mentioned here, so we are to assume that he probably had already passed away.

The celebration is in full swing, and everyone is having a wonderful time. But then, a major colossal social embarrassment is about to happen. The groom ran out of wine! Listen, if there was anything that the groom had spent a whole year proving, it was that he could take care of this bride. He built her the house. He acquired all the materials and demonstrated he had what it takes to take care of her for the rest of her life. To run out of wine is such a horrible oversight that it bought embarrassment and shame to the family.

Can you imagine what the bride's father was thinking? If you have daughters, you know what I am going to say. Our biggest fear is that our daughter is going to marry some loser. Right? Some guy we have no clue if he even can get a job and make a living. Some bloke who utterly petrifies us because he cannot suitably take care of our precious little girl. I mean, is this guy just smoke and mirrors? Are there any good qualities in this guy? This guy at Cana ran out of wine during the most important celebration he would ever have in his life. What an embarrassment!

The Bible claims they ran out of wine, and I know some would argue that wine is not like how wine is today. They will claim that the wine back then was not alcoholic, that it was basically grape juice. I mean, there is no way that the Savior of the world, God in the flesh, would serve over 120 to 180 gallons of alcoholic wine to these people. I mean, wine is the devil's plaything! Alcohol is evil!

However, the reality is that wine was a staple drink in the ancient world, and they made it from all kinds of fruits, though mostly grapes. Plus, there was no refrigeration back then, which meant that the juice was subject to fermentation. When juice becomes fermented, it turns to alcohol. So, on the one hand, quenching your thirst with just water could be dangerous because the water was not purified, and you could get sick. But on the other hand, if you just drank wine, you might get drunk and go streaking in front of your neighbor's house. So the way they dealt with it was that they diluted the wine with water. In Homer's Odyssey, it is said that they mixed it with twenty parts water to one part wine.[2] Pliny the Elder, a Roman author and a commander in the Roman Empire, mentions a ratio of eight to one.[3] Athenaeus's The Learned Banque, writes in a play around 200 A.D. that the custom was to mix three parts water with one part of the wine.[4]

Regardless of how much water they used to dilute the wine, they did this for several reasons. First, they could easily drink the water because the wine has now purified it. Second, they could now drink the fermented wine without getting hammered because it was watered down. And lastly, by watering down the wine, it lasts a lot longer.

Of course, there was straight-up unmixed wine as well, but the vast majority would dilute it with water.

"When the wine ran out, the mother of Jesus said to him, 'They have no wine'" (John 2:3). Question: why would Mary go to Jesus for help? I mean, Jesus is not from Cana. Mary may have known the wedding party, but she was also not from there. Do you think Mary knew Jesus would do a miracle? Maybe, but it doesn't make sense to me simply because Jesus hasn't done one before, at least that we know of. I think it would be better to assume that Mary just knew Jesus. It would be a fair evaluation that Joseph has already died, so who did Mary turn to when she needed help? Who did she turn to when she needed a solution to a problem? Can we just agree that Jesus has never had a horrible idea or come up with a wrong solution? Never once did Jesus lead Mary astray. Never once did Jesus lead Mary in the wrong direction. He had the perfect answer for every difficulty. He had the ideal answer for any mess. Everything that ever went wrong in Mary's life, Jesus would know why it went wrong and how to make it right. He was the most intelligent, knowledgeable, and resourceful person who ever lived or will ever live on this earth. Why in the world would Mary not go to him? I would, wouldn't you? Not only that, Mary knew that Jesus cared for and had great compassion for all people. She knew he would care for this groom who was making a complete fool of himself for not having enough wine. Who else would Mary go to? Who else equaled Jesus?

"And Jesus said to her, 'Woman, what does this have to do with me? My hour has not yet come'" (John 2:4). The word "woman" is not a negative term. It would be like us saying, "Ma'am." This is, however, the first time Jesus says the phrase *"my hour has not yet come."* He says it a lot in the Gospel of John. He will say it in John chapter 7, chapter 8, chapter 12, chapter 13, and chapter 17. Every time it is in reference to Jesus looking toward the fullness of the cross and the hour of his death and resurrection. What Jesus is saying

is that what I am about to go and do from this point forward will be divinely directed by God, and it will ultimately end in my death.

This means every event and occurrence leads to that final hour that God is determining. So to say my hour has not come, Jesus is reminding Mary that this situation in Cana is outside of God's timetable.

Now Mary was chosen to be the mother of the Son of God for many reasons, but one of them is because she was highly intelligent. Jesus said, my hour has not come, and in all her wisdom, Mary nodded her head and turned away. "Okay," she says. She then immediately tells the servants, probably with Jesus standing within hearing distance, *Do whatever he tells you"* (John 2:5). So slick. I am convinced that all mothers took a class on shrewdness somewhere! You got to love Mary. Sure, Jesus, whatever you say. I guess it is on the divine timetable now!

Now the story begins to speed up. *"Now there were six stone water jars there for the Jewish rites of purification, each holding twenty or thirty gallons"* (John 2:6). That would be around 120- or 180-gallons total. *"Jesus said to the servants, 'Fill the jars with water.' And they filled them up to the brim. And he said to them, 'Now draw some out and take it to the master of the feast.' So they took it"* (John 2:7-8). The servants filled up these giant jugs with water. Once completed, they got a ladle and took some of the water, now turned to wine, to the master of the feast, probably the groom's dad. He sampled the wine that used to be water and was blown away by how good it tasted. I do not know when the miracle happened, probably somewhere between the white spaces of verses 7 and 8, but this is massive.

How do you get wine? You gather a bunch of grapes. How do you get the grapes? You need vines. And how do you get the vines? You need seeds. How do you make the vines grow? You need to bury them in the earth and need sunlight and water. Once you have the grapes, you will need to crush them and strain them to get the juice. But what we see here in this miracle is no seeds, no vines, no sunlight, no earth, no water, nothing! Jesus just created wine out of nothing! And what is outrageous is that he gives it no fanfare whatsoever. Can you imagine how awesome that wine must have tasted! I am not much of a wine drinker, but yes, please!

The master of the feast was blown away. What is this deliciousness? At this point in the seven-day wedding, most people distribute wine that is diluted 1 to 10, but this—this—is unbelievable! Yes! The party is back on!

IS IT TIME?

The apostle John proclaims, *"But these are written so that you may believe that Jesus is the Christ, the Son of God, and that by believing you may have life in his name"* (John 20:31). If you want to know why Jesus was at the wedding at Cana that is it. It is why he did the miracle and turned the water into wine, and it's why he did every one of his miracles. It is why he had such compassion for people and why he loved them so much. He did it all so that people would come to believe in him.

> ## JESUS IS MY HERO BECAUSE HE CANNOT WAIT TO BE WITH ME, HIS BRIDE

Throughout the Bible, Jesus is referred to as the Bridegroom, and we are his bride. With what we know about the ancient Jewish marriage, consider this for a moment. The bride price has already been paid, and God paid that through the sacrifice of Christ on the cross. Paul will say in 1 Corinthians 6:20 that we have been *"bought with a price."* With the price settled and the sacrifice made, the bride and the groom come together. Sinful humanity joins hands with the holy Christ. The cup has been offered, and if we take it, we are forever his, and if he takes it, he is forever ours. After we take a sip, declaring our love for each other, and with the formalities over, Jesus heads back home to prepare a place for us.

"In my Father's house are many rooms. If it were not so, would I have told you that I go and prepare a place for you? And if go and prepare a place for you, I will come again and will take you to myself, that where I am you may be also" (John 14:2-4). Think about this for a second. If Jesus could create wine from water without ever saying a word, how quickly do you think it would take him to prepare a place for us? A second? Maybe two? He is like a young lover longing to be with his bride, counting down the seconds until he can be with her.

Unfortunately, Jesus hasn't come back to take us to be with him, so the time has not yet come. Matthew will add, *"But concerning that day and hour no one knows, not even the angels of heaven, nor the Son, but the Father only"* (Matthew 24:36).

I can imagine Jesus acting like me on my wedding day. On my wedding day, I couldn't wait for the wedding to start.

"Is it time yet?"

Only for the pastor to say, "Not yet, Scott. It's not time yet."

"Why the wait? I long to be with her!"

"I know."

"Let's hurry this up? I want to see her. I cannot wait to be with my bride!"

Jesus is my hero, not only because he is the lover of my soul, but because he is infinitely more in love with me than I could even conceive. He cannot wait to be in my presence and share his life with me. I don't know about you, but that moves me beyond my core and makes me want to be more and more like him. What kind of God longs to spend time with a sinner like me? I cannot wait for him to come back and take me to be with him.

John, who was with Jesus in Cana, got a small glimpse of what being with Jesus would be like. He pens:

> Then I heard what seemed to be the voice of a great multitude, like the roar of many waters and like the sound of mighty peals of thunder, crying out, "Hallelujah! For the Lord our God the Almighty reigns. Let us rejoice and exult and give him the glory, for the marriage of the Lamb has come, and his Bride has made herself ready; it was granted her to clothe herself with fine linen, bright and pure"— for the fine linen is the righteous deeds of the saints. And the angel said to me, "Write this: Blessed are those who are invited to the marriage supper of the Lamb (Revelation 19:6-9).

This picture from John is like a young Jewish son after completing his house, going to his dad, longing for the marriage feast to begin.

"Is it time yet, dad?"

"Not yet, son, but soon!"

"It cannot get here soon enough!"

"I know son, and when the time comes, blessed are those who are invited to the marriage supper."

"Dad, I cannot wait."

"I know, me too!"

"It's going to be awesome, isn't it? They will love it, won't they?"

"More than they will ever know!"

Something to Think About...

1. What is Jesus' main purpose in coming into our world and living as a man? Is his purpose to perform miracles and help young newlywed couples, or something more?

2. Jesus made over 100 gallons of wine in an instant! When Jesus does miracles, does he just barely meet the minimum, or does he provide abundantly? What does this tell you about Jesus and his relationship with us?

3. Why do you think John chose this miracle when there were thousands to choose from?

4. If Jesus could turn water to wine in a heartbeat, how hard do you think it would be for him to prepare a place for us in heaven? Why do you think he is still waiting to come and get us? Do you think there is something we are to do or become that is delaying him?

5. What does it mean to you when you realize how much Jesus wants to be with you?

9

CHAPTER

I'll Take Your Only?

❖

LOSING MY PAST AND MY FUTURE

Despite our racial makeup, or cultural background, or where and how we grew up, there are two things all people in this world have in common. Number one, we all are made in the image of God, and number two, we will all experience pain and suffering. There is no amount of money one can have, corporate position one can climb, or fame and attention someone may get, they will experience pain. It doesn't matter if Jesus is your hero or not, we will all experience pain and heartaches. It comes from sinners living in a sinful world, and no one is exempt.

I remember getting a phone call on a Saturday morning in August of 1992. I was sixteen years old, and I am not sure why I picked it up. We didn't have cell phones back then so I had to get out of bed and go and pick up the phone that was permanently attached to our kitchen wall. I was not a Christian then, so sleeping in on the weekends was sacred to me, and I was a staunch disciple devoted to those precious hours worshiping my bed.

"Hello?"

"Scott, you need to pack a bag, your brother Andy was in an accident, and we need to fly to Indiana."

"What?

"Just pack a bag; I'll pick you up in five minutes. Our flight leaves in two hours."

Click.

It was my dad, and he sounded panicked, which made me panic. My dad is a model of calm and coolness, even in the midst of trials. Not very often did my brothers and I see him lose his cool. My head was spinning. What happened, and how bad is my brother hurt? When I was three years old, my parents divorced, and our dad got custody of Andy and me, but when my brother hit fourteen, he moved in with my mom in Indiana. We were seventeen months apart and two peas in a pod growing up, so it hurt deep when he moved away. All I could think about was if he was okay or not. I had no answers, and it was maddening.

When dad picked me up, he packed quickly, frantically grabbed what was needed, and the next thing I knew, I was cruising at thirty thousand feet, heading toward one of the worst days of my life. I picked up bits and pieces of what happened and learned that my brother was heading to work, riding his motorcycle, when a car swerved and forced him off the side of the road. To make matters worse, they were expanding the road, so it was under construction. The car forced Andy to veer off the road where his motorcycle hit a large pile of gravel. His bike launched into the air and ejected him off the motorcycle. His bike landed about fifty feet beyond the gravel pile. Andy landed about fifty feet beyond that with his helmet lying about fifty feet further. Most of his internal organs were damaged beyond repair.

At the hospital, we learned that there were not much the doctors could do to save him. My dad had to decide what no father should ever have to make when it comes to their children. He agreed to take Andy off life support. We all had our special moment to say goodbye, and about an hour later, he passed away. The funeral was two days later, and we buried him in a cemetery a thousand miles from where I lived.

If you have ever lost a loved one, you would know what I was going through. Every emotion seemed to lump together as dark clouds hovered over my head. I went from sad, to depressed, to angry, to completely numb. The finality of losing my brother was suffocating. One night, I remember lying in bed crying out to God, telling him I hated him for taking away my brother. The overarching question that I demanded, but was never answered, was: WHY! Why God! Why did you take my brother? He was only seventeen; he had his whole life ahead of him! Why? Why God? WHY!!

Pain is devastating!

Fast forward, my wife and I are in Iowa interviewing for a job as a senior pastor. I was getting burned out as a student pastor and knew I would kill a kid if I had to do another middle school lock-in. Honestly, I believe that middle school lock-ins are an invention created by the Devil himself to torment God-loving student pastors. As we were in Iowa interviewing, my wife was seven months pregnant. I remember one night she had a look of concern on her face. She looked at me and said, "I haven't felt the baby move in a while." I didn't know what to say to that, so I replied, "It should be okay. Maybe he is resting." What did I know? I never had to carry a baby in my belly for nine months. However, never underestimate a woman's intuition. Her look of concern worried me, but I was trying to play it cool.

We flew back to Texas the next day, and she got an appointment to meet with our doctor the following morning. I had a meeting with one of our church members whose child was in my student ministry, and Charlotte was okay if I didn't go with her. I remember my wife calling me in the middle of a deep conversation during this meeting. I decided not to answer because I didn't want to interrupt this dad. Yeah, I can be a real insensitive fool sometimes. In hindsight, I would have answered it immediately.

About twenty minutes later, as I was walking to the car, I listened to the message my wife had left. I could tell she was trying hard to hold back the tears, but in essence, she said I needed to come to the hospital; she was in one of their waiting rooms waiting for me. I got in my car and called her.

"Hey, what's up? How's our baby, Elijah?"

This time she allowed the tears to roll.

"We lost him."

"What?"

"The doctors are saying that he is no longer breathing."

"Okay, hold on, I will be right there! We will get through this!"

"I don't know what happened! Scott, what happened?"

"I honestly don't know. I will be there in twenty minutes. Babe, I am so sorry!"

I am not sure how fast I drove, but I was flying! I couldn't stand it that Charlotte was all alone when this devastating news broke out. When I arrived at the hospital, all the nurses knew who I was and why. They all gave me sympathetic looks, whispering to me and giving directions to where Charlotte was waiting as if whispering was going to soften the blow. When I entered the room, Charlotte and I embraced for what seemed like an eternity. Since the baby was seven months along, Charlotte would have to be induced into labor. We were allowed to go home that night but returned early the following day. Some of our friends took our two other children to have some alone time to process, pray and be with each other.

They say when you lose a loved one, you lose the past. When I lost my brother, Andy; I couldn't help but be constantly reminded of the memories my brother and I shared. But over time, those memories slowly begin to fade if not frequently reminisced. We lose our past. But when you lose a child, you lose the future. We couldn't help but talk about what our son would be like in the future for seven months. Was he going to be a preacher like his dad, or the next Top Model, like his mom? All of that was taken from us in a blink of an eye. Our first two pregnancies had no complications, so we were not only bewildered by this but also devastated.

Pain is peculiar because it can leave some overwhelmed and immobile while others seem to learn to move on and adapt quickly. I have felt both, and I hated both. No one wakes up one day and says, "Boy, I would love to have my heart wrecked today, so I can stay in bed for months, not wanting to see or talk to anyone!" In addition, no one wants to move on quickly after a loss and try to adapt when everything in you is screaming to dig a hole and crawl in it. Plus, the guilt of moving on makes us feel like we are losing them forever.

REST IN PEACE, JOHN

I know that you and the billions of people on this planet have gone through similar situations where you were shrouded by pain, loss, and overwhelming sadness. Again, life plays no favorites. We all will go through moments of pain. This chapter, however, is not meant to exegete the Bible and try to solve the mystery as to why God allows us to experience pain and suffering. Rather, I want us to see how Jesus handled pain in his life and what he taught his disciples amid the hurt. If this doesn't make Jesus a hero, I don't know what will.

> *Now when Jesus heard this, he withdrew from there in a boat to a desolate place by himself. But when the crowds heard it, they followed him on foot from the towns. When he went ashore he saw a great crowd, and he had compassion on them and healed their sick. Now when it was evening, the disciples came to him and said, "This is a desolate place, and the day is now over; send the crowds away to go into the villages and buy food for themselves." But Jesus said, "They need not go away; you give them something to eat." They said to him, "We only have five loaves here and two fish." And he said, "Bring them here to me." Then he ordered the crowds to sit down on the grass, and taking the five loaves and the two fish, he looked up to heaven and said a blessing. Then he broke the loaves and gave them to the disciples, and the disciples gave them to the crowds. And they all ate and were satisfied. And they took up twelve baskets full of the broken pieces left over. And those who ate were about five thousand men, besides women and children.*
> (Matthew 14:13-21)

This passage comes when the news of John the Baptist's death hit Jesus and the disciples hard. Jesus found out that his cousin, John the Baptist, was beheaded. John and Jesus were close. In Matthew chapter 11, Jesus says that there is *"no one greater than John."* The news of losing him was tough (Matthew 11:11).

In Mark chapter 6, King Herod invited all his high and mighty friends to join him in his birthday bash. Much alcohol was served. Amid their drunken stupor, Herod's brother's wife, Herodias, whom Herod married, used her daughter to seduce Herod and all his friends. When they are all drunk, this daughter begins to danced seductively and entertains them. Herod was so pleased by the entertainment that he told her that he would grant her whatever she wanted. So, she went back to her mom, Herodias, and said, "What should I ask for?" Herodias, without even blinking, said, "The head of John the Baptist" (Mark 6:24). She was bitter because John insisted that Herod should never have married her.

Herod, not wanting to look bad in front of all his friends, ordered John's head to be put on a platter and given to this girl. How you could let your daughter be a part of something so grotesque is unfathomable to me! There are no boundaries when evil is concerned. News of this traveled fast. When Jesus and his disciples heard about John, they planned to get away from the busyness of doing miracles, healings, and ministry and spend some R&R to regroup. *"Now when Jesus heard this, he withdrew from there in a boat to a desolate place by himself"* (Matt 14:13).

How did Jesus handle the pain? It says that in one of Jesus' most painful moments, he withdrew. He withdrew? I find that interesting because I just assumed that Jesus never withdrew amid the pain. Or, for that matter, never withdrew from anything. We see him being harassed all the time by religious leaders, yet he never withdrew. There were so many attempts to kill him, yet he was never bothered and kept doing what he was doing. We see him at the cross, and he didn't withdraw; he faced it head-on and received it. But not here. Here he tells his disciples, we need some rest. If you read the Gospel of Mark, it will say that their schedule was so busy sometimes that there were occasions when they didn't even have time to eat (Mark 6:30-31). Everyone wanted Jesus' time and attention. With the news of John's death, Jesus called a timeout and told his disciples, let's go! Let's pause and head to a desolate place where we can process this news and grieve together.

But when the crowds heard it, they followed him on foot from the towns (Matt 14:13). Wouldn't you know it, as soon as they made it to their destination vacation, all these people showed up. I mean, before they had the chance to set up their recliners on the beach and catch some rays and waves, word got out.

"Hey, I just saw Jesus!"

"Where?"

"He was soaking it up on Laguna Beach!"

"Nice! Let's go!"

The Bible says that Jesus and the disciples get to their vacation spot, hurting and needing physical rest. Suddenly, people with significant needs show up and begin to put more demands on Jesus. Of course, Jesus sees the multitude of people, knowing they all came with their own pain, and he couldn't help himself. He was moved with compassion. *When he went ashore he saw a great crowd, and he had compassion on them and healed their sick* (Matt 14:14). Think about this, Jesus was physically weak and grieving. Yet, he extends himself and begins to minister to them all day long. Are you kidding me! I can imagine Peter (he was always the fiery one) saying, "Do you people even know what we are going through right now! Our friend was just murdered. We are hurting, and we are broken! Can you just leave us alone for one day! Seriously, just give us one day!"

No rest for the weary.

Let me give you another side note because I believe Jesus wants to teach us a valuable lesson here. You and I have experienced pain. Most of us have experienced pain on multiple occasions. Maybe you are reading this right now, and you are going through one of the worst moments of your life. We all have pain, and I am in no way trying to demean your pain; I am just saying we all have it. If we all decide that we will just wait till the pain subsides, you and I might be waiting for a very long time. Pain seems to be constant for most of us. However, some of the most significant moments in my life came when I was hurting and in pain, and God used my pain to minister to someone else in *their* pain.

Notice what Jesus is expecting from his disciples. He expects them to minister to this crowd, literally moments after John was buried and while they are on vacation to get away from it all and grieve. A vacation, by the way, that they greatly needed. I can imagine the disciples' frustration when forced to minister in such pain.

Now when it was evening, the disciples came to him and said, "This is a desolate place, and the day is now over; send the crowds away to go into the villages and buy food for themselves" (Matt 14:15). I love that this is in the Bible and I totally get what they are doing here. I can imagine all the disciples coming up to Jesus and the conversation went something like this:

Peter saying, "Hey Jesus, great talk, buddy! Very inspirational. Look, can we be done now? These people look hungry."

Andrew piping in, "Yeah, Jesus, all of them are hungry?"

Peter continues: "Yes, Jesus, all of them. We talked to all of them, and everyone said they are hungry and would like to go home."

Andrew adds: "Don't forget the woman and children. All of them too!"

Peter keeps going: "Yep, they want to go home too. I mean, look at those kids over there. They are getting restless. It's been good, Jesus. Let's call it a day."

I can imagine Jesus smiling at them with that kind of smile that communicates that I know something you don't. It probably made them nervous.

"Why is he smiling?"

"I don't know, but I don't like it!"

"Me either."

"Jesus, why are you smiling. You should be too tired to even smile."

Jesus looks them in the eyes and says, *"You give them something to eat"* (Matt. 14:16).

Andrew was like, "Peter, what did he say?"

"I am not sure, but it sounded like he said he wants you to feed all these people."

"Me! Why me? Peter, ask him if he is serious."

"Jesus, are you serious? Come on; we are beat! We are exhausted, and quite frankly, we are hurting because of the loss of our friend. Just send them home. Please."

Jesus answers them, *"They need not go away; you give them something to eat"* (Matt. 14:16).

"Yeah, but we only have five loaves of bread and a couple of fish. How in the world are we expected to feed all these people with that!

More than likely, that smile on Jesus' face returned. He knew that this was going to be a moment that they would never forget.

GIVE ME YOUR ONLY

These disciples were not only in pain of losing a friend, but they were exhausted. They have been riding the Jammin' For Jesus Train for a couple of years now, and it has been a non-stop roller-coaster ride from day one. And now, when they are finally going somewhere to rest, grieve, and relax, over five thousand people show up demanding attention, and Jesus tells them to feed them. You can imagine that they wanted to tell Jesus: "No!" I would. Sorry, Jesus, but I am wiped out. If this were me in this situation, I would say the most famous words in all of churchdom for getting out of doing something: *I'm burned out.*

If most Christians would say they were burned out in front of these twelve disciples, I know the disciples would laugh in their faces. Are you burned out? Really tiger? Burned out, huh? So what? Serving at your church for a little over an hour a month wiped you out? I am so sorry to hear that; here, take my towel and spot on the beach and lay in the sand. You deserve it.

I know these disciples are looking at those five thousand people, who didn't include the women and children, and they wanted to tell Jesus no. But they are smarter than me, so they immediately went back and proclaimed with great fanfare, "Sorry Jesus, we don't have the money nor the resources to be able to feed this many people financially. With only two fish and just a handful of bread, it is numerically unfeasible, so let's call it a night, and we can get back to our vacay first thing tomorrow!"

Things go from bad to worse. *Then he ordered the crowds to sit on the grass* (Matt 14:19).

Imagine this scene playing out. What do you think would happen if you are in a place with over 5000 people and are tired and burned out from serving all day—rather—all year. You realize it is getting late, and you cannot wait for everyone to go home, when all of sudden, someone in your group shouts out, "Everyone sit down!"

"Woah, what are you doing, buddy?

"SIT DOWN, EVERYONE! MY FRIENDS HERE ARE GOING TO FEED YOU!"

"What! No, we are not! Have you lost your mind?"

"WE HAVE PREPARED SOME FOOD FOR ALL OF YOU!"

"NO! NO! NO! No, we didn't! Five loaves and two fish! Please stop!"

"EVERYONE GRAB A SEAT. WE WILL PASS OUT THE FOOD MOMENTARILY."

Visualize the disciples in this story. They are emotionally, physically, and spiritually drained. They thought Jesus wanted to withdraw, and now they are in the throes of another Jammin' For Jesus Train revival.

What in the world is Jesus thinking? More to the point, why is Jesus getting more energized the longer this keeps on going? When Jesus called the disciples over, I can imagine one of them saying, "Jesus, what are you doing?" Jesus ignores it and begins to take some of the fish and bread and give each disciple a little bit. "Um, okay! What do you want me to do with this?"

Taking the five loaves and the two fish, he looked up to heaven and said a blessing. Then he broke the loaves and gave them to the disciples, and the disciple gave them to the crowds (Matt.14:19).

Of course what is left out is the disciples on the way to giving the little crumbs to the people, grumbling to one another.

"Are you kidding me? How will this feed five thousand people, let alone five people! We only have a piece of fish and some breadcrumbs."

"Jesus told us to trust him."

"Look, I love Jesus, but this is ridiculous! We only have..."

Matthew 14:17 says *"They said to him, "We only have five loaves here and two fish."*

I can picture the disciples getting more and more frustrated. They had to think that everything Jesus was working so hard for would go up in flames when they could not deliver on what he promised. However, they obeyed and began distributing what they had, probably thinking they would run out before even getting to the second row of people. Before they even knew what was going on, a miracle began to unravel in the palms of their hands.

In a place of pain and sorrow.

In a place of exhaustion and fatigue.

In a place of frustration and grief.

They witnessed, from their own hands, a miracle.

And they all ate and were satisfied. And they took up twelve baskets full of the broken pieces left over (Matt 14:20). It looks like Jesus delivered after all.

JESUS IS MY HERO BECAUSE HE WILL TAKE THE LITTLE THAT I HAVE AND USE IT, EVEN WHEN I DON'T THINK IT IS ENOUGH

Notice how the disciples said, *"We only have"* (Matt 14:17). Hey Jesus, we only have—we only—and yet Jesus will take the "only" you have and use it. Do you know what Jesus requires of us? He requires us to give him what we have right now. Jesus doesn't demand what we think we will have, or what we are working on having, but what we have right now. In the Sermon on the Mount, Jesus made it clear that we should not be *"anxious about tomorrow, for tomorrow will be anxious for itself"* (Matt 6:34). In other words, all Jesus cares about is today, not tomorrow. Tomorrow will take care of itself. Just take the only that you have today and give it to Jesus and see what he will do with it.

What is your only? Some of us are like; I don't know; I am exhausted right now. I am not even sure I can give Jesus ten minutes of my time. Others may be in so much pain because of a loss that they are not even sure if they can give Jesus five minutes. But here comes Jesus, invigorated and so full of life, not worried that all you got is a little piece of fish and some crumbs. He will take whatever you got and take care of the rest. I cannot tell you how many Christians I know think if they cannot give Jesus all the things that he deserves, it would be better not to give him anything. If I cannot give him what he is worth then what is the point? I don't want to give him my scraps; he is not worthy of that!

So, we wait. Maybe when I am fifty and my money-draining, life-draining children move out of the house, I will have more time and more energy to give to Jesus! Or when I am seventy and, retired, boy, how much I will be able to give him then! But right now, there is no way. Right now, I only have a few crumbs of bread and some stale fish, and that is not worthy of Christ. But one day, you just wait, Jesus!

Our hero, Jesus, says, give me what you have and let me determine what I can do with it. So often, we tend to think that Jesus is demanding every single day and hour of our lives and that if we cannot give that to him, he will turn his back on us. NEVER! Jesus will take one minute of your time, if that is all you have, just to be able to spend it with you! He will take the little we have and use it, even when we feel so unusable.

Jesus is my hero because I have never felt more profound satisfaction in my life than when I am with him. The moment I signed up to follow him, I faced some difficult and dark and some excruciating days. Still, I have always found such peace and satisfaction when he is with me, even during all that. I promise you, if there was a better way, or an easier way, where I can find more purpose, meaning, and satisfaction elsewhere, then sign me up. But I have never found it!

Life is too short. It is challenging and full of pain and doubt, yet it can bring excitement and thrills like no other. But because life is fleeting—here today and gone tomorrow—I don't want to get a little excitement here and there; I need real hope, authentic faith, and a fulfilled life. I want to make the most of the days I have left and live them on purpose. So, I double-dog dare you to do something this week. I dare you to give Jesus what you have and then see what happens. I dare you to give him the only that you have and watch; you never know; you may just see a miracle happen in the palms of your hands. What I do know for a fact is that when we give Jesus our only, he can radically and wholly change our life.

Those twelve disciples who were supposed to be on vacation grieving the murder of their friend ended up doing some unbelievable things in their lives. Except for one, the rest of the disciples were murdered similar to John the Baptist. In fact, they found it a privilege to die that way! They were forced to deny Jesus and all of them said, "No way! He is my hero!" Some burned alive, others crucified, but all died because of their love for Jesus. What kind of faith and commitment is that? That is more than just a dozen men trying to be moral and good so that they could feel righteous in and of themselves. No, these are men who were overwhelmed by the love of Jesus. Their love for him was so profound and significant that they were willing to die for it. They realized that life was not about money, status, or things and opinions, but their hero Jesus. They learned to lean into him, trust him with the little they had, and in the end, they found a life worth living and a hero worth dying for, even during pain.

Jesus knows we cannot give him much nor give him what he is truly worth, and that is why he will only ask for our only. Not yesterday's only, not tomorrow's only, but todays. I genuinely believe that if we give him the only that we have today, there is an excellent possibility he may do a miracle through us!

Something to Think About...

1. How often do you withdraw when things get rough? In Matthew 14:13-21, we see Jesus withdrawing when he heard about the news of John the Baptist. What does it mean to you that in moments of pain and brokenness, Jesus withdrew? Do you believe it is good to withdraw sometimes?

2. It is said that people will not care what you say until they know that you care. How was Jesus when it came to caring for people? How are we when it comes to us caring for people

3. Most Christians only look at what they can do. But in Christ, it is not what we see we have or can do; it is what He can do with what we have. Do our vision and thinking limit us?

4. What makes Jesus a hero is that what he requires of us is what we have today. He doesn't expect anything from us tomorrow or when we have all our stuff together. Just what we have today. What do you have today that you can give to him?

10

CHAPTER

Taking the Plunge

———◆———

TODAY IS THE DAY

I moved around a lot. Too many times to count. Well, I did count, but you would not believe me if I told you. My dad was in finance, and he had a headhunter on speed dial pointing out all these great opportunities where he could continue to climb the corporate ladder. For the life of me, I cannot remember how many elementary schools I attended growing up. I do know I went to four junior highs and two high schools. In my seventh-grade year alone, we moved from Georgia to New York, to Seattle and back to Georgia. It was brutal. Not only did I have to learn how to make friends quickly (if I did make any friends), but I also had to take almost every known state history class in all of America. I want to throw up thinking about it. It was brutal.

Georgia seemed to be our home base. Every time we moved somewhere, we found ourselves moving back to Georgia within a couple of years. One time, living in Alpharetta, Georgia, we lived in a huge neighborhood with an Olympic-sized pool and a separate diving area. To top it off, it had a high dive! I know that the high dives have disappeared from neighborhood pools as quickly as music videos from MTV, but at that time, at that glorious pool, we had one! The high dive was a monstrosity of a beast that begged to be conquered as a young teenager. It was alluring and scary, and it gave me the best shot of getting one of the hot girls who sunbathed next to the diving boards. If I could master the high dive, my cool factor would go up, and maybe I would make some friends. Since it was the summer, and we just moved, I didn't know anyone.

My brother Kevin and I would often go the pool. At first, we just got familiar with the boards as we jumped off. Over time, we learned how to do front and backflips off the low dive. It progressed to a flip and a half, to gainers, a double flip, and a bunch of other twists and turns that would blow my back out for months if I did them now. After mastering the double flip off the low dive, my brother and I thought it was time to try the double off the high dive. I was the youngest of four boys growing up, so I assumed my older brother would take the lead on this. NOPE!

"Scott, it's time!"

"For what?"

"The double on the high, you ready for it?"

"Maybe."

"Today is the day, and I want you to go first."

"Me! Why me, you're better at it?"

"I just feel you can nail it! You got this, little buddy!"

"Whatever!"

"TODAY IS THE DAY!"

What a bunch of crock! He was nervous and didn't want to go first. It just so happened that the girl I knew would be my third wife was sunbathing that day, and I went for it. I climbed up the steps, walked to the end of the board, tested its bounce, and then walked back for a running start. Was I scared? You betcha! Was I going to do it? Well, my mind was saying yes, but my quivering legs were in a profound protest. After what seemed like forever and several screams from the bottom of the stairs telling me to hurry up, I noticed that my soon-to-be girlfriend was watching me. I did a quick prayer, hoping it would be her that would give me CPR if things went sour, and I went for it!

Just a quick physics lesson for you: Front flips rotate at a much faster rate than any backflips can. This is done by inertia thrusting our bodies forward, and we can tuck faster and harder than going backward. In a backflip, the tuck is initiated much later. In a front flip, the energy used, also known as conservation of angular momentum, is more significant going forward than backward. In other words, the moment I leaned forward and tucked my legs into my chest, it was game over. I was done!

I ran like the devil was chasing me down the length of the diving board. I timed my jump perfectly and got in the air at a height I had never reached before. I instinctively tucked and grabbed my knees, placing them up to my chest as I started to lean forward. I thought I heard the ooh's and ah's from the bystanders below. I imagined I was in the Olympics.

It was magical.

It was glorious.

I got this!

Those thoughts lasted about half a second. I quickly knew that I was too high and rotating too fast and that things would not end well. I was committed, though, so I kept the tuck formation and saw nothing but sky, water, sky, water, at a rate that left me dizzy. To make a long story short, I didn't do two front flips on the high dive—I did two and a half flips! Take that, Kevin! Unfortunately, it did not end with my arms hitting the water first in an outstretched diver's position. Instead, it was my face! Hard. I saw it coming with just enough time to clench every muscle in my body and close my eyes.

Have you ever hit the water at such a high velocity that it forces your eyes open? I would not encourage it. I hit that water going about Mach 10 with more rotation than a bullet zipping through the air. Newton's third law states that every action or force in nature has an equal and opposite reaction. My face was the equal and opposite reaction. It hit that water so hard my clenched eyelids didn't stand a chance. The chlorine-induced water became like icepicks stabbing out my corneas. It may have been the most physically painful experience in my life. I couldn't breathe, mainly because my brain decided to take a timeout and forgot to tell my body that I needed to swim to the top for air. It jarred my body so hard that nothing seemed to work anymore.

I finally made it up for air. I couldn't tell if everyone was watching me or not; my eyes decided to take a vacation with my brain, and it left me to fend for myself. I did hear my brother say, "THAT WAS AWESOME!" I guess my ears were still working. I swam to the side and collectively took a breath while assessing the pool to see if any of my major organs were floating around somewhere. My brother decided that this day was not the right time to try the double flip on the high dive. Chicken! Nor did that girl become my third wife—or girlfriend—or even friend. Shame!

Did any of you have the fortune of spending a good bit of time on the water? I loved it. I was at the neighborhood pool almost every weekend. Many life lessons can be found there. For example, the bottom of the pool does not smell like strawberries. Yeah, I know; I bet you always wondered that. I was about twelve, and some high school kid came up to me and said, "Dude, the bottom of the pool smells like strawberries." I knew this kid to be a bully, as he bullied me often, so I played it off and acted like I already knew that. He was disappointed in my reply and eventually swam away, but it got my brain to think. Does the bottom of a pool really smell like strawberries? Only one way to find out. I went to the bottom of the pool and used my hands and feet to get my face as close to the bottom as I could get. I took in the most extensive breath I could take, trying to sniff the pool floor and evaluate if the pool smelled fruity. Sure, I practically filled one of my lungs with water and almost drowned, but I did learn a valuable life lesson that day: Don't listen to bullies! They are all fools!

Now that I am a dad of three children, you would think we would spend most of our weekends at the pool. Currently, we live in a large neighborhood where there are about twenty pools of all shapes and sizes to choose from. Some have diving boards, others are with slides, but unfortunately, for my kids, I stay away from the pool like the plague. I do this mainly because the heat in Texas can melt your skin. When I was a kid, the temperature never bothered me, but now I am much older (and hairier!). I sweat just thinking about sweating—not a fan. But I am not a monster, so eventually, I will take my kids to the pool. I yell at them before they all scatter and do their thing that we are not staying long, so you better swim fast! I quickly gauged where the nearest shade was to park myself there while trying not to perspire through all my clothes. I know; you probably would think I could get in the water where it was cool. Sure, I could, but now my white pasty skin seems to be allergic to the sun. When I was younger, I used to tan, but now all I do is get burnt like a piece of toast.

Occasionally, my kids will yell at me to jump in and play with them. It's funny when you think about it because when I was their age, I would just jump in and feel nothing but summer bliss. Now I am the guy who slowly wades into the pool. I am the old man who must take, small tentative steps into the pool as I slowly acclimate myself to the pool's temperature. Before, I would do a belly flop to get in. Now I am the guy who looks like he had an epileptic fit the more I put my body in the water. It's sad, which makes me sad. I have officially become the old guy at the pool that my younger self laughed at.

This next story of Jesus will show us that sometimes being the old guy and wading in is not an option. More often than not, when we follow Jesus, we just need to jump in feet first. This story will hopefully teach us that by taking the plunge, the heroic nature of Jesus will become crystal clear.

TAKING THE PLUNGE

Being a pastor for over twenty years, I can say that the Christians who get frustrated the most are the ones who try to wade into their relationship with Jesus. Those tentative steps after tentative steps in their faith and relationship with Christ can be such a time drainer. Not only that, but it can also get very unsatisfying trying to tiptoe our way into a life with Jesus. No! We need to understand that our relationship with Jesus should be an adventure. It is not about trying to play it safe. I honestly believe it is almost impossible to play it safe and at the same time follow Jesus. In Matthew 14, we get a glimpse of this.

> *Immediately he made the disciples get into the boat and go before him to the other side, while he dismissed the crowds. And after he had dismissed the crowds, he went up on the mountain by himself to pray. When evening came, he was there alone, but the boat by this time was a long way from the land, beaten by the waves, for the wind was against them. And in the fourth watch of the night he came to them, walking on the sea. But when the disciples saw him walking on the sea, they were terrified, and said, "It is a ghost!" and they cried out in fear. But immediately Jesus spoke to them, saying, "Take heart; it is I. Do not be afraid." And Peter answered him, "Lord, if it is you, command me to come to you on the water." He*

said, "Come." So Peter got out of the boat and walked on the water and came to Jesus. But when he saw the wind, he was afraid, and beginning to sink he cried out, "Lord, save me." Jesus immediately reached out his hand and took hold of him, saying to him, "O you of little faith, why did you doubt?" And when they got into the boat, the wind ceased. And those in the boat worshiped him, saying, "Truly you are the Son of God" (Matthew 14:22-33).

Jesus and his disciples spent all day ministering to thousands of people. Jesus is tired. The disciples are wiped out. And the night has approached. This would be a good time for them to play it safe and say, "Hey, Jesus, why don't we just hunker down here for the night and move out tomorrow!" The Bible says that Jesus immediately made his disciples get in a boat and begin rowing to the other side. Now, what is that? Is that jumping or wading? Jesus expects his disciples to get in the boat and start rowing. There is no wading in here. He didn't explain to his disciples what would happen that evening. No one gave them instructions. There was no breakdown of what the night might bring. There was no explanation that this night was going to be somewhat alarming. There was no mention of a lot of rain and wind and total darkness enveloping their rickety little boat. There was not a word from Jesus letting them know that every single one of them would be scared out of their minds.

NOPE!

There is no heads up! It's get in the boat; let's go!

After watching his disciples get in the boat and start rowing to the other side, Jesus goes up to a mountainside and begins to have some alone time. He is praying and regrouping after a grueling day. The Bible says that a massive storm appears while those twelve disciples are huffing and puffing, barely able to keep their eyes open. Of course, Jesus sees this, and so he gets up and walks (on the water) towards them.

This leads to a fascinating "get-to-know-you" question. Which scenario would you least like to encounter: 1). Being caught in the middle of the night in the middle of a storm on a tiny little boat thinking that the storm will capsize your boat and you drown? Or 2). Watching what you believe is a ghost walking on water in the middle of the night during a storm where you are confident that this ghost will kill you? I haven't decided which one is worse, I would probably be scared out of my mind either way!

I have heard so many sermons on this passage that it is hard to read it without those voices in my head. Of course, every pastor who preached this passage must focus on the storm, right? So, let's look at it. Who caused this storm? I can remember a pastor explaining how this storm is because of our own doing. No doubt his intention was good. I mean, as Christians, we are good at saying that the reason why storms come out of nowhere and ruin us is that we were not following Jesus the way we should! Yeah, I know you are going through a tough time in your life right now, but to be fair, your life would be different if you were actually following Jesus. Oh, you lost your job? Glad I am not you. If you had gone to church more and read your Bible the way you should, I bet you would have been promoted and not sacked.

Could it be that this storm inundated these twelve disciples because it was just the rainy season, and no one was at fault? Could it be that storms will come to all of us simply because life plays no favorites? Storms will come; the only difference is will we face them head-on, or will we cower in the back of the boat, hoping the rain won't touch us?

Peter is one of the guys you just have to root for and love. Peter is a guy who will jump feet first into a storm without realizing the consequence of what he does. He is impulsive and very passionate. Peter will come up with some emotionally foolish things, and then Jesus will make him do them. You got to love Peter! Here comes Jesus walking on water as if he is some model strutting his stuff on a runway in Paris, and all the disciples lost their minds. It is the fourth watch of the night, which means it's after 3 am. The disciples are mentally and physically wiped out, and out of the corner of their eyes, they see what appears to be a ghost coming right for them. The Bible says that they all cried out. And to be fair, you would too! I know I would! Jesus tries to calm them down by screaming out, *"Take heart; it is I"* (Matt 14:27). To which Peter replies, "Prove it!"

Again, you got to love Peter's passion!

They all think death is knocking on their doors from both sides. On one side, the storm is a doozy, but on the other, the ghost is no laughing matter either. Then they hear the familiar voice of Jesus saying, *"Do not be afraid"* (Matt 14:27). Jesus exclaims he is here with them in this storm. And then Peter goes and opens his mouth!

"Jesus, is that really you? If that is you, prove it! Tell me to come and walk on water with you!"

"COME!" (Matt. 14:29).

"Ah…I'm such a fool! What did I just get myself into!"

I am pretty sure Peter was getting out of the boat during one of the worst storms he has ever encountered, thinking, "I am a fool, Peter! This is dumb! Why did I open my mouth?"

Now, let me ask you another question. If you were to walk on water, how would you do it? To be clear, this is just a hypothetical question. Peter and Jesus are the only two people who have ever walked on water. For the record, this story has nothing to do with walking on water. It has everything to do with our hero Jesus. But, if you were to walk on water, how would you do it? Keep in mind this is not water from your neighborhood pool or the crystal-clear water off the coast of the Caribbean where it is smooth as glass. This water has produced massive waves after massive waves during a downpour caused by a mighty thunderstorm.

I will tell you how you would walk on this type of water. Every step would be deliberate. Every step would be planned. Every step would be calculated. Every step would be supernatural. Every step would be "OH SWEET JESUS!!! Oh, wait! I'm good—I'm good! I'm still floating on the water! I'm still alive!"

Every.

Single.

Step.

When it comes to Jesus being our hero, there will be times when you will have to get out of the boat and get wet. There will be times when you will have to take the plunge and try the double flip off the high dive. There will be times when you will get soaked. There will be times when you will have to say to yourself that you can no longer wade into this.

WHY DO YOU DOUBT

The Bible stated that he began to sink when Peter saw the wind and the rain. Jesus immediately grabs him and pulls him back up. No doubt there was panic in Peter's eyes, and with compassion, Jesus said, "O, *You of little faith, why did you doubt.*" (Matt 14:31). It is an excellent question from Jesus and one in which Christians get wrong all the time. I think there are a lot of Christians who believe that doubt and faith are irreconcilable. Faith and doubt are not allowed to co-exist. If you believe in Jesus, you should never doubt! Doubt is for the faithless. Doubt is for those who are not followers of Jesus. Doubt is for the faint of heart. Reread that sentence from Jesus again. "*O, You of little faith, why did you doubt.*" Just from that sentence, Jesus is saying you can still have faith and doubt going on simultaneously. Our hero Jesus is not intimidated by our temporary doubts. We all have them, and Jesus knows we have them.

The picture here is Jesus as a loving father holding his child when that child was afraid of something that he shouldn't be. I cannot tell you how often my kids slept with us at night because they were afraid of the dark. I would always tell them, don't be silly; the darkness cannot get you; it's the evil monsters lurking in the dark you need to be watchful of! Not sure why our kids slept with us so much!

Jesus is holding on to Peter, like a dad holding onto a son who lost confidence. Jesus noticed that Peter's faith was getting smaller and his doubt was getting bigger. What's the deal, Peter? Why are you doubting? I mean, both Peter and Jesus were literally walking on water here. *O, You of little faith, why did you doubt.* It's an honest question by Jesus. We don't know Peter's answer because it is not given to us, but I am sure that if Peter were honest with himself, he would have said, "Why do I have doubt, Jesus! Really? I mean, look around!" Notice this conversation is going on during the wildest storm that Peter has ever encountered in his life. Jesus could have easily calmed the storm and then had a pleasant conversation about his doubt. But no, he let the wind and the waves go wild amid this conversation.

Why did you doubt, Peter?

Truthfully, it was because he looked away from Jesus. When he walked towards Jesus, his eyes were on him, all good and well. But the moment his eyes left Jesus, everything went downhill fast. Jesus knew that Peter wasn't missing anything, and if he just kept his focus on Jesus, everything would have been fine. Peter, now soaking wet, is probably thinking, "Yeah, thanks, Captain Obvious!"

I wonder if some of the doubts we may face are because we decided to get out of the boat and get soaking wet! Is it where we are not playing it safe anymore? Is it where we decided we would take the plunge and follow Jesus no matter where it led us? Sometimes we find ourselves in a storm thinking, did I make the right choice? This doesn't look so safe anymore. I wish I'm not so wet!

One of the most significant inaccuracies of being a follower of our hero Jesus is that we think we are supposed to show up at church all dry, and the goal of our lives is to live it where we never take the plunge and get all wet. So, we hang around all our non-wet friends, sing Kumbaya and praise Jesus that we are so dry. I see this all the time in church. Men and women come in with their hair all done, wearing their Sunday best as if there was no care or worry in the world. Most put on their plastic smiles because heaven forbid anyone sees them off their game. It seems to be the mindset of many Christians in our culture today. I am just going to play so I can stay dry. I mean, I don't want anyone to see me at church all wet and a mess.

Can you imagine if the goal of Christianity was just to stay dry? We would have all these pastors telling their congregation members to get in the boat and stay there!

"Alright, people, let's get in the boat and hunker down!"

"Why?"

"Great question—well, we are going to stay here in this boat because we are going to do some great things in our community, and by staying dry, the world will know who we are!"

"Yeah, but the storms are hitting our communities pretty bad."

"Sure, but when the storm passes over, then we can reach them!"

"Yeah, but don't you think it might be a good idea to get out of the boat? You know, to let other people know that we are here."

"Well, I am not sure? I mean, if we go out in the storm, it might get ugly. Plus, we will get our nice Sunday clothes all wet. We definitely don't want to do that! Can you imagine that! How irreverent!"

Before we know it, our motivation to get out of the boat is based on fear and not faith. So we will hunker down in our nice dry little boat, and we can boast to all our Christian friends about going to our dry church and about how proud we are for staying dry. Man! I didn't even get wet this week! I am so godly.

Lame!

Let me ask you something: whose faith is more exciting in this story, the guys in the boat or the one who risked it all by getting out of the boat? Sure, Peter stumbled a little bit, but at least he was willing to get out of the boat. All of us would say that Peter is the one who had a more exciting time. Who wouldn't want to walk on water with Jesus!

After the conversation with Peter on the water, during the storm, Jesus helps Peter back on the boat, and it is there that he calms the storm. Most scholars will say that the disciples know that there is something special about Jesus at this point. Still, they don't fully understand how special he is, and they don't know he is the Son of God. But this storm becomes a turning point for them.

Jesus is now in the boat, he calms the storm, and all is peaceful, and these disciples are like—you are him! Listen to the awe and wonder of what they say in verse 33. *"Truly you are the son of God"* (Matt 14:33).

The disciples, and especially Peter, learned a precious lesson here. More often than not, you and I can see Jesus unlike any other place than when we see him in the storms of our lives. Sure, we may hate the storms, and there is no guarantee that Jesus will calm those storms, but he will walk with you through them. In the end, we may say that it was awful and we hated almost every minute of it, but if we are willing to get wet, I promise you we will say we saw some of Jesus that we have never seen before.

And it was amazing!

No matter how hard we try not to get wet, we will all face storms in our lives. Some of us will cringe and try to hunker down and stay dry. But the rare few who attempt to keep their eyes on Jesus and get out of the boat may experience Jesus in ways one could never have dream or imagined. One thing is sure, though, you and I will never see Jesus as a heroic figure if all we ever want to do is play it safe and remain in the boat all dry.

ASLAN, THE LION

Do you remember the book (or movie), *The Lion, The Witch, and the Wardrobe?* C. S. Lewis wrote several books, which became the Narnia series. *The Lion, The Witch, and the Wardrobe* became the second in this series (although it was the first movie). Lewis wrote these children's books to show a parallel of the struggles and victories of our own Christian life.

If you have any kids, buy the books and read them to your children. It is well worth it.

In *The Lion, The Witch, and the Wardrobe*, Susan and Mr. Beaver are talking, and Mr. Beaver is trying to explain to Susan who Aslan is. In one of C. S. Lewis' last letters before his death, he wrote of how Aslan was a picture of Christ. He wanted to use a lion because Jesus was called the Lion of Judah in the Bible. He also added that he wanted Aslan to be a lion because the lion was supposed to be the all-powerful king of beasts.[1]

The scene plays out like this:

Susan: Who is Aslan?

Mr. Beaver: Why you don't know? He is the king and the lord of the whole wood.

Susan: Is—is he a man?

Mr. Beaver: Aslan a man! Certainly not. Aslan is a lion—*the* lion, the great lion.

Susan: Ooh! I'd thought he was a man. Is he—quite safe? I shall feel rather nervous about meeting a lion.

Mr. Beaver: Safe? Who said anything about safe? 'Course he isn't safe. But he is good.

He's the King, I tell you.[2]

I think C. S. Lewis could not have explained our hero Jesus any better. Jesus is like that lion. Yet, for most, we like to think he is just a man—a safe man. What? No one said anything about being safe! Jesus is not safe, but he is kind, and he is King indeed.

You and I were born on this earth to truly live. We were born to get out of the proverbial boat and make a difference in our lives and impact our neighbors' lives. To let the world know that Jesus is our hero. Sure, we may get soaked, and there may be some doubts that come our way when the storms are blowing, but my hero, my King, my Jesus; he is kind, and he is right in the middle of the storms with us. However, the more we try to play it safe, the more we will fail to see what Jesus is capable of.

> JESUS IS MY HERO BECAUSE NO MATTER WHAT HARDSHIPS OR STORMS COME MY WAY, JESUS IS ALWAYS IN THE CENTER OF IT WITH ME

Where was Jesus in this storm? Right in the center with his disciples. Go back to verse 27 of this text. *"But immediately Jesus spoke to them, saying, 'Take heart; it is I. Do not be afraid"* (Matt 14:27).

The words *"It is I"* are just two words in Greek (*ego eimi*), which means "I AM."[3] I know that doesn't necessarily mean much to us, but the "I AM" statements of Jesus are a direct declaration of his deity. When God commanded Moses to go back to Egypt to set his people free, he was conversing with God. He asked him, *"Indeed, when I come to the children of Israel and say to them, 'The God of your fathers has sent me to you,' and they say to me, 'What is His name?' what shall I say to them?"* God replied, *"You shall say to the children of Israel, "I AM has sent me to you"* (Exodus 3:13-14). In other words, God's name of "I AM" is the all-inclusive, irrefutable identifying name of our creator God.

The disciples of Jesus are stuck amid the storm of the century. They are terrified, thinking they are goners, and here comes Jesus, right in the middle of it with them, declaring that he is the creator God himself right there with them. It is truly a decisive moment.

Maybe some of you are going through a terrible storm in your life right now. Where is Jesus in this storm? If you are like me, there are times when I am like; I have no clue where Jesus is! The winds and rain are too strong! Why is this not safe! Why do I have to go through this! Why is this so hard! I constantly scream out:

WHERE ARE YOU? I CANNOT SEE YOU! THE WINDS AND RAIN ARE TOO MUCH AND I AM AFRAID! I DON'T KNOW IF I CAN KEEP GOING ON! I HAVE SO MANY DOUBTS RIGHT NOW! I DON'T FEEL SAFE!

Yet, every time when my focus is on Jesus, I know he is there with me, helping me get through this storm together. Knowing he will never let me go and showing me a part of himself that I have never seen before. Every time, through every storm, Jesus shows me time and time again a part of himself that I never knew before.

When Jesus and Peter finally got in the boat, those twelve young followers of Christ saw what Jesus was truly capable of. *"Truly you are the Son of God!"* (Matt 14:33). I—I have never seen anyone like you before. You're—You're amazing! Are you safe?

No one said anything about being safe! But Jesus is kind, and he is King indeed.

So often, we tend to forget the Bible passage that states that Jesus will never leave us nor forsake us (Hebrews 13:5). As for me, Jesus is my hero because no matter what kind of storm comes in my life, he is right there in the middle of it with me. *"Take heart; it is I"* (Matt 14:27). The all-powerful creator God is right in the middle of my storms, and I wouldn't want it any other way! Quit playing it safe, and let's get out of the boat and see what Jesus is capable of!

Something to Think About...

1. After reading Matthew 14:22-33, why do you think Jesus allows us to go through storms? In what ways has your trust in Jesus strengthened or challenged you during storms in your life?

2. Does it bring you any comfort that Jesus is fully aware and cares about what you are going through?

3. Going forward in obedience is always better than going backward in disobedience. How easy would it have been for the disciples to turn the boat around and go back to shore? What would they have missed if they went back?

4. How often do we allow our doubts to creep in amid storms, and we lose sight of Jesus' goodness and power? Do we believe that storms in our lives have the potential to open our eyes to the power of Jesus?

5. Do you believe that the storms in your life have the potential to open the eyes of other people to the power of Jesus?

11

CHAPTER

Time to Fight

———◆◆———

DEATH MOUNTAIN

Fight or flight? Which one are you? If something unexpected happens, what are you going to do? Will you fight or take flight? You can learn a lot about someone's faith by whether they choose to fight or high-tale it in flight. The hardest part is figuring out who is a fighter or who is a flighter. You never really know until something happens, and they have to make a split-second decision to choose. Most people will surprise you with what they choose. Also, most people take flight rather than fight.

My grandparents grew up in the hill country of Huntington, West Virginia. If you have never been there, it is a lovely place to visit. At least once a year, my dad would take us to West Virginia to see them, which allowed my brothers and me to hang out with our cousin, Steve. Steve was a gangly little boy who grew up into a six-foot-six giant of a man! But back when we visited him as kids, he was all arms and legs and a motor that would never stop running. We would play in the woods, hunt for imaginary creatures, and have sleepovers where forts were built and pillows were destroyed in fights. It was some of my favorite times during the summer.

When I was seventeen, my grandfather passed away, and we all flew out to West Virginia to pay our respect and be there for our grandmother.

As you get older, the only time you get a chance to catch up with family is usually during weddings or funerals. This was one of those occasions. I hadn't seen Steve in about five years, and I was excited to connect with him again.

After the funeral, my brother Kevin and I went out with Steve to grab some food, and we went to—umm—well—a wing restaurant that rhymes with "looters." We were enjoying the wings and the overall ambiance of the place (wink-wink) when Steve leaned over and looked Kevin and me in the eyes and said, "You want to go to Death Mountain?" Well, I didn't see that coming. Okay, I am intrigued. I mean, I am an immortal seventeen-year-old; of course, I wanted to go!

"What's Death Mountain?"

"It's a place where people go to worship the devil or something like that."

"Sweet, let's go!"

Keep in mind I was not a Christian at the time, so don't judge me.

Steve told us all the rumors that gave Death Mountain its name as we drove there. You know, the typical stuff of human sacrifices, ghost sightings, and, of course, the screaming of unknown people being tortured that can be heard when you are on the mountain. Looking back, I am confident that I didn't believe a word of it. As we exited the freeway and started going up the mountain on a gravel one-lane road, nervousness flowed through my body. It was pitch dark and close to midnight, with a waning moon that didn't help at all. OKAY, fine! I was a little scared!

As we approached the top of the mountain, Steve rolled all our windows down to listen if there was any screaming people being tortured before we fully committed. No doubt he was probably cracking himself up every time he looked at my wide-eyed stare in the rearview mirror, thinking how gullible I must be. The gravel road became a narrow dirt road, and it was very narrow, our car almost hitting the trees. Finally, we made it to the top, and there before our eyes was a large clearing and an old, dilapidated barn of some type. The barn had graffiti all over it, mostly of anarchy signs and, of course, several pentagrams. We saw no other cars or people anywhere, so we parked by the barn, and all of us got out of the vehicle.

Someone painted a bunch of red paint on the only surviving door of the barn. At least, I was hoping it was red paint. Beyond the barn was this eerie light that appeared as if something or someone was right behind the barn. My imagination was getting the best of me because I could have sworn I heard voices in the distance. Unfortunately, I believe my brother Kevin heard it too because he whispered to us, "I don't think we are alone up here."

Have you ever had goosebumps on top of your goosebumps? No joke, this was a very creepy place. It was as if I could feel evil in the air. I was ready to leave the minute I got out of the car.

But then it got worse.

As Steve, Kevin, and I were walking to the backside of the barn where the weird light and voices were, we heard a car approaching. It's now past midnight. Who in their right mind would come up to this god-forsaken place! We are all frozen in place. Was it really a car? Were our imaginations getting the best of us? NOPE! It was a car, and it was coming towards us.

Fight or flight?

Steve looked at us. Kevin and I were looking at Steve. Finally, with panic in his voice, Steve yelled, "Run to the car!"

Flight it is!

Now, a little bit of info on my good ol' cousin, Steve. He is a legit killing machine. I cannot remember the name of the karate he took for years, but if you could go beyond the black belt, he was there. Many martial arts paraphernalia were in his back seat of the car as we rode up to Death Mountain. He had two sets of nunchucks, several throwing knives, and a twelve-inch-long metal rod with a pointed top. I guess you could jab someone in the spleen with it if you wanted to. Who knows? The point is that he knows how to fight and how to fight to win. He once showed me this move called the Praying Mantis, and with just one finger, he had me on the floor in pain with tears in my eyes. I'm not playing; he had to register himself with the state of West Virginia to let the world know he was a living, breathing, killing machine. This means if anyone decided to be dumb and pick a fight with him, Steve was legally obligated to declare at least three times that he knew karate before he engaged in a fight. Otherwise, he could go to prison if that person was severely injured. He is one nasty dude!

Until the mysterious car came up the hillside, Steve was upbeat and having a good time. No doubt, he was laughing inwardly at our expense. But now, his eyes showed fear, and when he told us to run to the car, you don't question his killer logic, you run!

I was the first one to the car. I thought my awesome black parachute pants made me run like the wind in eighth grade, with all the zippers and pockets. Ha! Nothing like fear to make you become like Usain Bolt! I tried to open the door, but it didn't budge. I tried again but it still wouldn't open.

"STEVE! THE DOOR WON'T OPEN!"

"What?"

"THE DOOR WON'T OPEN!!"

"I know; I locked the doors."

"WHAT!!"

We are in the middle of Nowhere, West Virginia, with no cars in sight and no human life around, and my cousin decided this was the best place to lock his doors when we all exited the car! What did he think someone would rob his vehicle while we were investigating the other side of the barn? Dumb!

Kevin and I were at the car waiting for my prudent cousin to unlock his beat-up Corolla that would probably only rake in about $200 on the black market. Steve may be six foot six and a legal killing machine, but that boy runs slow! Finally, with the doors unlocked, we all bolted into the vehicle, and I yelled out, "LET'S GO!"

But then it got worse.

The car would not start.

I kid you not! The engine sounded like the noise I made when I decided to see if the bottom of the pool smelled like strawberries. I felt like I was in some cheap horror film where I knew we would end up leaving the only safety we had and be forced into the old barn where the evil monster lurked in the dark corner, ready to pounce! Needless to say, I was now clutching that twelve-inch spike, thinking to myself that I was not going to go down without a fight! You won't siphon out my soul tonight, witches!

"This ain't funny, Steve! Start the car!"

"I'm trying!"

"Try harder!"

True panic was now in Steve's voice. Maybe all those stories leading up to the mountain were real. I grabbed one of the nunchucks in my other hand, just to be sure.

Finally, the car started, and Steve gunned it, sending dirt everywhere. As he turned the car around to go back down the mountain, we saw the other car's headlights shining through the trees. I honestly have no clue how we would navigate this because that road was very narrow. Steve didn't think it was a problem because he gunned it down that road as trees blurred past, inches from the car.

A minute later, we come up to the mysterious car. Both cars must slow down and get off the road as much as possible to pass each other. To not hit the trees on either side, both cars are now going about two miles an hour to pass each other. It's as if we were going in slow motion. Sweat was beginning to bead down my forehead, fear gripped my heart, and my hands were clenched tight on weapons I had no clue how to use.

As we were passing the car, I noticed that Steve wouldn't even look in the direction of the other car. His head was straight as an arrow, probably thinking, if I don't see you, you don't exist. On the other hand, I was sitting behind Steve on the same side as the car we were passing, and I couldn't help but look. I mean, what kind of fool would go up to Death Mountain after midnight on a random Thursday. Other than us, of course.

Have you ever seen the movie, Interview with a Vampire? The guy driving the car looked like Lestat, played by Tom Cruise. It was unnerving. As we were slowly passing each other, Lestat, the vampire, slowly—ever so slowly—turned his head and looked right into my eyes. Our eyes were locked on each other for what seemed like an eternity. It may have been the creepiest thing that has ever happened to me. I couldn't help it; I broke the eye contact with the blood-slurping vampire and yelled out to Steve, "GUN IT! GUN IT! HE SAW MY FACE! I'VE BEEN MARKED!" The weirdest part of it all was that there was no one else in the car with this guy. He was all alone!

After we made it safely down the mountain and headed back to my grandmother's house, we had a good laugh about it. But one thing was sure, my cousin Steve failed us. Here was a living, breathing killing machine, and when the first sight of trouble came, he caved like the rest of us. Kevin and I are not trained killers, so we get a pass when we happen to scream like a high-pitched middle school girl while running to the car. But Steve was just as panicked. He should have been the calm and cool one. He should have said, "Don't worry boys, I got you! No one will steal your souls tonight! Not on my watch!" But no, Steve was a mumbling bumbling chicken like the rest of us!

I forgive him, though, and he is still one of my favorite cousins!

WHAT ARE YOU MADE OF

Have you ever been stretched to the limits to see what you are made of? It can be highly beneficial. Often, we have no clue how far we can go, how strong we are, or the limit of our potential, until we have been stretched to the breaking point. I would assume most of us will never know, more often than not. Usually, we don't like how it feels when we get stretched. We don't like bending till we come close to breaking. For most, we would instead enjoy the status quo than go beyond ourselves to see what we can do. Many a times, we would rather be shallow than go deep.

I'll be honest, I usually break. Looking back, I cannot tell how many times I gave up. Maybe it was because of fear. Or perhaps it was uncertainty. But more times than not, it was because I didn't want to go the extra mile. I gave up the fight too early, and I never saw what I was truly made of. When it comes to fight or flight, I often pick flight. Wait, is that a deranged vampire coming up the mountain? Flight! What, you want me to lift a ton of weights to look good? Flight! Are you saying that I must work hard to achieve my goals? Flight! No one ever told me that marriage would take a lot of work. Flight! And so on.

This next story of our hero, Jesus, will show us a woman who was determined that she was ready to fight for what she wanted when it came to choosing between fight or flight. And Jesus let her. We will see that when Jesus becomes our hero, there will be times he wants us to choose fight over flight. Check it out:

> And Jesus went away from there and withdrew to the district of Tyre and Sidon. And behold, a Canaanite woman from that region came out and was crying, "Have mercy on me, O Lord, Son of David; my daughter is severely oppressed by a demon." But he did not answer her a word. And his disciples came and begged him, saying, "Send her away, for she is crying out after us." He answered, "I was sent only to the lost sheep of the house of Israel." But she came and knelt before him, saying, "Lord, help me." And he answered, "It is not right to take the children's bread and throw it to the dogs." She said, "Yes, Lord, yet even the dogs eat the crumbs that fall from their masters'

table." Then Jesus answered her, "O woman, great is your faith!
Be it done for you as you desire." And her daughter was healed
instantly (Matthew 15:21-28).

Jesus had less than a year before he faced the cross. With all the political and religious pressures being put on Jesus, he took his disciples to the district of Tyre and Sidon. It would be about 50 miles north of Israel in what we call Lebanon today. This is a deliberate withdrawal to get away from everyone and everything and spend some time with his disciples as he prepared them for life after his death and resurrection. Clearly, he did not go there to minister to people because he *"entered a house and did not want anyone to know"* (Mark 7:24). However, our hero is always approachable, available, and interruptible.

And behold, a Canaanite woman from that region came out
and was crying, "Have mercy on me, O Lord, Son of David;
my daughter is severely oppressed by a demon (Matt 15:22).

If you know anything about the Canaanites, they were the original occupants of the Promise Land. When God sent his people into the Promise Land, he ordered all the Canaanites to be destroyed (Deuteronomy 7, Joshua 6). The Canaanites were neither innocent nor ignorant of God; instead, they constantly rejected him and were a corrupting influence in that land, so God wanted them purged. However, the Israelites did not eradicate all of them. The only reason why this woman was alive to encounter Jesus was that the Israelites were disobedient.

I say all that to clarify if there were anyone outside the covenant of God, it would be this woman. She was an outcast and a sinner from a people who were sinners. In the eyes of the Israelites, she has no claim and no right to the covenant of God or his love and mercy. To the Jews of that time, she had no worthiness to ask Jesus for anything.

Fight or flight?

Do I go to Jesus and fight for my daughter, or do I take flight at the first sign of resistance when Jesus doesn't tell me what I want to hear? You can tell a lot about someone when all the chips are on the line. No doubt, she went to all her gods and idols, praying and hoping for a miracle. But when nothing happened, she reached the end of her rope until Jesus came to her town.

Matt 15:22: *"Have mercy on me, O Lord, Son of David; my daughter is severely oppressed by a demon.*

She ascribes Jesus with two titles here. *Lord* and *Son of David*. One highlights a sovereign deity, and the other dignifies the promised Messiah and savior. This is not a woman casually saying, "Excuse me, sir." No, this woman is coming with humility and respect. It was probably quite refreshing for Jesus since most of the Jews in Israel constantly called Jesus a drunk, or friends of sinners, or that Jesus himself was demon-possessed. From the disrespect of the hateful people back home, Jesus encountered the respect of this hated Gentile. It's a beautiful contrast.

Whether or not this woman believed in Jesus' lordship or messiahship, she at least came to know that this man had supernatural power that could help her daughter. Indeed, Jesus will drop everything and help her.

> *But he did not answer her a word* (Matt 15:23).

Umm—Jesus? Really? I thought you were always approachable? I thought your love for people was irrational? I thought you would always come running even when we are a long way off from being in a perfect relationship with you? What's the deal? Such an un-Jesus-like thing to do here, Jesus.

Fight or Flight? What are you made of?

Jesus had it up to his eyeballs with all the superficiality and triteness back in Galilee. So much shallow soil and weedy grounds. What we are seeing here for the first time is Jesus putting up barriers which this woman must fight through to show the reality of her faith. Jesus is preparing his disciples for things to come; he doesn't have time to surround himself with more people of weak faith. If this woman wants something from Jesus, she will have to fight for it. So, Jesus says nothing.

> *But he did not answer her a word. And his disciples came and begged him, saying, "Send her away, for she is crying out after us"* (Matt 15:23).

The disciples are like, "For the love of all that is holy, Jesus, send this woman away! She is doing nothing but crying, yelling, and wailing at us!

Just heal her already so we can get on our way!" This, by the way, indicates that Jesus was silent for a significant amount of time.

"Jesus, can you help my daughter?" Silence.

"Please, Jesus, I need your help." Silence

"JESUS! HAVE MERCY ON ME!" Silence.

I can imagine Peter leading the charge to silence this woman and send her away. "Come on, Jesus, you have healed thousands of people. Heal her and be quick about it because she is getting on my nerves! Plus, we are here to get away from the crowds, if she keeps this up, people will notice, and then there goes our little private retreat!"

Jesus finally speaks.

> He answered, "I was sent only to the lost sheep of the house of Israel" (Matt 15:24).

That has a slight sting to it. You have to ask why this passage is even in the Bible if you think about it. Jesus keeps on doing a bunch of unlike Jesus-type things. Imagine someone saying to this woman, "Sorry, I cannot help you. You are not Jewish, and I only came for the Jews." That is the equivalent of someone coming up to me, whom I do not know, asking for my help, and I reply, "Yeah, sorry. You are not a member of my church, so I cannot help you, nor do I care what your needs are."

Ouch!

I can imagine this woman standing there with her mouth open and eyes unblinking as she hears the words that just came out of Jesus' mouth. I know that would have been me! I probably would have gotten mad at such a flippant disregard for my pain and misery. Maybe I would have said a very snide remark as I walked away. Perhaps I would have been too crushed even to move as I watched Jesus and his posse walk away, thinking my daughter would never be cured. One thing is certain, I would have let Jesus walk away, and I would have tucked my tail and left.

Fight or flight?

Jesus, on the other hand, is testing this woman's resolve. He is testing her faith. He wants to separate her from all the shallow faith he has seen all around Israel. And this woman does not disappoint. What she is made of is pure steel! She is a fighter.

But she came and knelt before him, saying, "Lord, help me"
(Matt 15:25).

What makes this woman's faith probably more remarkable than mine
is that she never gave up. I will have great faith, and I will join the fight as
long as my pride doesn't get hurt along the way. I will fight as long as I know
I won't be humiliated. I will fight as long as my independence or freedom
doesn't take a hit. In other words, I will fight as long as I know I will win.
But this woman? She kneels before Jesus in great humility. She doesn't care
if her pride gets shot in the process. She doesn't care if she looks a fool in
the dirt before this man. She doesn't care. She was coming to Jesus, and she
would not let him leave.

And he answered, "It is not right to take the children's bread
and throw it to the dogs" (Matt 15:26).

Can we just assume that Jesus must have forgotten his coffee this
morning? I can imagine Peter saying, "Jesus! You are on a roll with this
woman!" Andrew might have been thinking, "Yo! Jesus! If you are trying to
convert this Canaanite woman, you are blowing it, buddy! Maybe you need
more rest. God knows we are all exhausted!"

At first, Jesus was silent. Then he said she wasn't Jewish. And now he
is calling her a dog! What in the world is going on here!

Fight or flight?

Jesus is putting up another barrier for this woman.

Do you remember when Lazarus was sick? Jesus could have come earlier,
but he waited. He waited until Lazarus wasn't even sick anymore because he
died. Like, dead—dead. Four days dead. Why did Jesus wait that long? In
John 11:15, Jesus says, *"for your sake, that you may believe."* He was testing
their faith. He does that a good bit in scripture. And he is doing it here.

Jesus is drawing out her faith.

He knew he would heal her daughter. He is always approachable and
available, and his love for all people never changes. But he is putting up
fences with this woman so she would have to fight and plow through them.

Sorry, but it is not right to take food from the table and give it to the
pet when it should go to the children.

*She said, "Yes, Lord, yet even the dogs eat the crumbs that fall
from their masters' table" (Matt 15:27).*

This is a fighter! She is sharp, takes Jesus' analogy, and goes a step
further. She is persistent. She doesn't know how to take flight or go down!
She will take whatever Jesus throws at her using it to fit her situation. I like
this woman.

*Then Jesus answered her, "O woman, great is your faith! Be
it done for you as you desire." And her daughter was healed
instantly (Matt 15:28).*

What faith you have! I cannot tell you how many times I long to hear
those words from Jesus, spoken to me in my prayer life. Seriously, think
about it. When was the last time you knew Jesus would have said that about
you? When was the last time your faith was so great that you knew Jesus
would have been smiling at you. "O woman! O, Man! Great is your faith!"
When was the last time? Was it last week? Was it last year? Has it been
years since you think your faith has been great?

Fight or flight? Which one are you? You can tell a lot about a person's
faith by how they answer that question. This woman was a fighter, and she
never backed down. She was willing to take everything that Jesus threw at
her without leaving her in defeat or despair.

BUNCH OF SNOWFLAKES

I am not sure who came up with the term "snowflakes" to address a particular
type of person, but I always find it amusing. It's like trying to insult a person
with the gentlest of all words. I know it is used primarily in the political
world, with the left slinging it at the right and the right hurling it to the left.
Still, I am not sure if there is a better word to describe Christianity in our
culture today. As followers of Jesus, most of us are a bunch of snowflakes.
As soon as we leave our comfy and safe little atmosphere and find ourselves
taking some heat for the God we love, we melt almost every time. Somewhere
down the line, we have forgotten how to take criticism. We have forgotten

that others' opinions are not a threat to our existence. We have forgotten that the world doesn't revolve around us. We have forgotten that our God often will make us fight for things to see what we are made of. And if we are a bunch of snowflakes, we will never know the potential and great faith we have, or what God will do through us because of it. Far too often, we melt at the first sign of resistance.

JESUS IS MY HERO BECAUSE HE WILL OFTEN STRETCH ME TO MY LIMITS TO SEE WHAT I AM MADE OF

I don't know about you, but I don't want a hero who will only tell me things to make me feel better about myself. I don't need a hero who sugarcoats issues so my feelings won't get hurt. I don't need a hero who tiptoes around specific topics lest I get offended. I don't need a hero who will just placate me. I don't need a hero who will try to soothe and pacify me.

No!! I don't need that, and neither do you!

We need a hero who will challenge us to be the best person we can be. Sometimes, it may not be pleasant, and there will be barriers that Jesus will throw in front of us to fight through.

Jesus will often stretch us to our limits so that we can finally see our true potential. Life is too short, and Jesus' mission is too vital for us to live our lives with such shallow, superficial faith. There are already too many such "Christians" filling every single church in America—we don't need more of them! There is a reason why Jesus left those people in Galilee to go to the region of Tyre and Sidon. The shallow and superficial Christians do no good to Jesus' mission. All they want is for Jesus to toss them a bone from under the table occasionally. They would rather be pacified than be forced to persevere when the heat turns up. Unfortunately, as we have seen in our culture, most melt.

I want a hero who will challenge me. I want a hero who will call me out when I don't live up to my expectations. I want a hero who sees the best in me, pursues me to be the best, and won't settle for less. That is what I see in Jesus in this story. Jesus made this woman the best person she could be—a person who found great faith in a hero—but she had to fight along the way to get there.

Something to Think About...

1. Fight or flight? Which do you choose more often? Why do you think that is?
2. Would you have been offended if Jesus or another person talked to you the way Jesus spoke to this Canaanite woman?
3. What did Jesus say about this woman's faith when she refused to give up? If Jesus were to describe your faith, what might he say?
4. How is this woman's response something we should do in our own life when we experience challenging situations?
5. How often has Christ tried to stretch your faith? Did you refuse to be stretched, or did you allow Jesus to take you beyond what you thought you were capable of? What happened in both situations?

12

CHAPTER

Ultimate Authority

———◆———

AUTHORITY ISSUES

When I was younger, I had authority issues. I cannot tell you why I had problems with authority; I just did. Some may say it was because I had daddy issues or mommy issues, but the fact is, my parents were great and loving yet strict and fair. I remember several times I got kicked off the school bus because I was not a fan of the bus driver telling me to sit in my seat facing forward. At the time, I thought that was a ridiculous rule that needed to be broken. Who cared about safety as long as I got what I wanted?

My favorite teacher in high school was my Spanish teacher, Ms. DiMingo. I lived in Alabama at the time, and she hadn't lived in the US for long, so her accent was thick, and she would always complain that our accents were too redneck. She never said that, but I am sure that is what she meant. I would constantly mess with her and use a ridiculous southern drawl when I was told to read a sentence in Spanish. *Meee Elephante esss muu-eee grande!* It would always drive her up the wall. But she was a hoot, and I enjoyed that she didn't take any of our high school drama too seriously. On the other hand, she was also not afraid to deal out punishment when things got out of hand. Do you remember how I was nominated, class clown? Yeah, my incredible sense of humor only went so far. At least a dozen times, she had kicked me out of class and made me sit in the hallway until she came and got me. I knew I was pushing her buttons. I knew I was always taking things too far. I knew she would punish me for my lack of respect for her rules. Yet, for some reason, I couldn't help myself. And she was my favorite teacher!

After about ten minutes, she would come out in the hallway and sit down with me. She would ask how things were at home or how I was doing in sports. I constantly disrespected her, yet I knew without a shadow of a doubt that she genuinely cared for me. She would end up saying, "You know, I have to call your parents and let them know what you did in class today, right?" "I know," I would reply. I had issues!

Later, I was a bagger at a local grocery store. The educational level you need to master the words "paper or plastic" was immense! This was back when people would tip you when you took their groceries out to their cars. I cannot remember the most significant tip I got, maybe five dollars, but I remember the lowest tip I ever got. I walked an elderly lady to her car and helped her put all the groceries in her trunk. She thanked me and then took out her coin purse from her bag and placed a penny in my hand.

A penny!

One cent!

With utmost sincerity, she looked me in the eyes and said, "This penny has brought me luck, and I believe you will need it, so I want to give it to you as thanks for taking out my groceries." I didn't know what to say, and I couldn't tell if she was being serious or if she was just being cheap. I smiled at her and went back inside.

The manager saw me walking back in and instantly thought I was goofing off and not bagging groceries. She may or may not have caught me goofing off a lot while I worked there, but that is not the point. The point is that the manager didn't like me, and I didn't like her. Later that day, she busts in the breakroom during my break and lets me have it. In no uncertain terms, she let me know that I was twenty minutes past my break time and should have been out front helping bag. Was she correct? Of course, she was. But I let her know in no uncertain terms that I quit! I couldn't stand her dictatorship in my life! How dare she tell me what to do! She replied something about a door not hitting me in a place where the sun doesn't shine.

I am not sure that was a lucky penny after all!

For most of my adolescent life, I had an authority problem. I had authority issues with my parents, teachers, bosses, police officers, and even my school librarian. Today, scientists will claim that authority issues result from control aversion in their brains. Science will call it "strong brain connectivity between the parietal lobule and the dorsolateral prefrontal cortex," which "commonly associates with attention reorientation and cognitive control."[1] Basically, you just want to rebel against anyone and anything that hinders your personal decisions and actions. I, on the other hand, like to say we are extremely selfish and anything that hinders our own selfish decisions and actions, we rebel against all day long. It doesn't matter if the people we disagree with have a list of degrees longer than that penny-giving lady's grocery list; we still think we know what is best.

The funniest thing I have seen lately was a sign I saw heading to my Airrosti guy to work on my shoulders (lame CrossFit!). I saw a sign on an office door at the medical center that said, "Please don't confuse your Google search with my medical degree." I love that! Sadly, people have to post stuff like that, but that is the culture we live in. We live in a time where we are the sole authority figure, and everyone else is second-hand at best. My opinions, decisions, and actions are the only things that matter, and if you don't like them, then shove off. I don't need you! Cancel culture is alive and well, even with Jesus' followers. That is why I truly believe this next story of Jesus is desperately needed for all of us.

THE GOOD CENTURION

When he had entered Capernaum, a centurion came forward to him, appealing to him, "Lord, my servant is lying paralyzed at home, suffering terribly." And he said to him, "I will come and heal him." But the centurion replied, "Lord, I am not worthy to have you come under my roof, but only say the word, and my servant will be healed. For I too am a man under authority, with soldiers under me. And I say to one, 'Go,' and he goes, and to another, 'Come,' and he comes, and to my servant, 'Do this,' and he does it." When Jesus heard this, he

marveled and said to those who followed him, "Truly, I tell
you, with no one in Israel have I found such faith. I tell you,
many will come from east and west and recline at table with
Abraham, Isaac, and Jacob in the kingdom of heaven, while the
sons of the kingdom will be thrown into the outer darkness. In
that place there will be weeping and gnashing of teeth." And to
the centurion Jesus said, "Go; let it be done for you as you have
believed." And the servant was healed at that very moment
(Matthew 8:5-13).

Do you want to know a little Bible trivia? Did you know that every time you see a Roman Centurion in the New Testament, that person is always a nice dude? It's true, and it's impressive when you think about it because there were some nasty centurions in Jesus' day. I love how God handpicks the most hated people in all of Israel to illustrate goodness and faith. It is almost as if God is showing us these people to let the world know about the extent of his kingdom's mission which is far beyond the reach of just the Israelites.

Here you have this man who was not only a Gentile but a Roman soldier to boot. He was a member of the occupation force of the Roman army who tried to suppress and oppress all of Israel. I can imagine the anger of the Pharisees upon seeing Jesus talking with a man of such stature. Why in God's name would you ever do a favor for somebody like that! But that is the point of Jesus, is it not? At that time, the religious leaders in Israel had no perspective on the parameters of God's kingdom. They thought that God's love and grace were only afforded to them. God's kingdom is confined to Israel, and here comes Jesus, and he blows that notion out of the water. If you want to know why the leaders in Israel refused to believe Jesus' authority and sought to kill him, it is because of stories like this.

Lord, my servant is lying paralyzed at home, suffering terribly
(Matt 8:6).

A couple of things here. We need to pull in Luke's account of this story to understand this passage. Matthew uses the Greek word, *Pais,* which means child. But in Luke's account, he uses the Greek word, *Doulos*, which means servant or slave.[2] This means that the centurion had a young slave who happened to be a child. In that culture, it was not uncommon to have a child slave, or child servant, in the house. For example, if you had a male and female slave, and they had a child, that child would end up becoming a slave to their master as well. Not saying I agree with any of that, but that was how it was back then.

This young child was paralyzed.

We don't know what caused this paralysis. It could have been polio, a tumor, or a disease in the nervous system. It could be that this child was healthy and had a fall and broke his back; we don't know. What we do know is that this centurion was a very caring man. He cared for this child servant. It would have set this centurion apart from the rest of the Roman world. During the reign of the Roman Empire, slaves didn't matter. If they suffered, it didn't matter. Whether they lived or died, it didn't matter. Enslaved people were of no consequence to the Romans. They were thought of as things, not humans.

Aristotle once said, "For master and slave have nothing in common: a slave is a living tool, just as a tool is an inanimate slave. Therefore, there can be no friendship with a slave as slave, though there can be as a human being: for there seems to be some room for justice in relations of every human being with every other that is capable of participating in law and contract, and hence friendship also is possible with everyone so far as he is a human being."[3] In other words, slaves are not even considered to be humans, and they are nothing but inanimate things. You were not allowed to be friends with a slave.

Gaius, a Roman law expert, once said in the *Institutes*, "We may note that it is universally accepted that the master possesses the power of life and death over the slave."[4] If a slave did anything to you, whether they looked at you wrong, or made your sweet tea too sweet, you had the right to determine if that slave would live or die. It was "universally accepted" that if you didn't like your slave—well—kill them.

Varro, a Roman writer, once said in his work *"Res Rusticae,"* (translated "Village Affairs"), which was more of a manual on how to handle your property or estates that slaves ran, said that "the only difference between a slave and a cart is that a slave talks."[5]

I use those quotes to let you know that back in Jesus' day, and especially with the Romans, slaves were nothing but tools and things. They were so low on the scale of importance that they weren't given the title of human beings. So, if your slave was paralyzed, you can imagine what a Roman would do. This child slave is now no good for anything. He cannot walk, and he cannot plow. He cannot move around and help around the house. He was useless. Get rid of him!

This centurion is a good guy! He is not like the rest of the Roman world, and he cared for this boy. So he goes to Jesus and says, "Jesus, my boy servant is paralyzed and in miserable pain. Can you help him?"

Matt 8:7-8: *And he said to him, "I will come and heal him." But the centurion replied, "Lord, I am not worthy to have you come under my roof, but only say the word, and my servant will be healed."*

It gets interesting here because you must pull in Luke's account to see what is going on. Luke says it like this:

> Now a centurion had a servant who was sick and at the point
> of death, who was highly valued to him. When the centurion
> heard about Jesus, he sent to him elders of the Jews, asking him
> to come and heal his servant. And when they came to Jesus,
> they pleaded with him earnestly, saying, "He is worthy to have
> you do this for him, for he loves our nation, and he is the one
> who built us our synagogue" (Luke 7:2-5).

This can get a little confusing because Matthew states that the centurion came to meet with Jesus, but Luke says that the centurion sent elders of the Jews to speak to Jesus. So whose account is correct? Did the centurion go, or was it the elders of the Jews? Most scholars would say that Luke's account is the correct one. However, Matthew is not wrong, either. Matthew just skips the middleman and gives us the meat of the matter. For Matthew, the words may not have come out of the mouth of the centurion, but they were still his words. What we can glean from these two passages is that: 1). The boy was not only paralyzed, but he was dying. 2). The centurion loved the Jewish nation and its people (as seen by the Jewish elders coming on his behalf). And 3). This centurion helped build the synagogue that no doubt Jesus has served and worshiped in. No matter how you interpret it, this is a good man wanting to help a child in need.

Do you want to know why the centurion didn't want Jesus to go to his house, even though the child was there? Because this centurion knew all about the Jewish ceremonial teaching passed down by rabbis. One of the teachings was that a Jew was not to contact anything touched by a Gentile, lest you become unclean.[6] The Jews declared all Romans unclean because of their worship of false gods and dealings with idols. Thus, all Gentiles were ceremonially unclean. If you met a Gentile and touched anything, you would become unclean and go through the purification rites to become clean again. This could last up to seven days.

This centurion knew that having Jesus in his house would make him unclean. It would force Jesus to spend up to seven days away from ministering and healing while he went to get clean, and he didn't want Jesus to violate that. So the moment that Jesus was about to head to this guy's house, he stopped him and said:

> But the centurion replied, "Lord, I am not worthy to have you come under my roof, but only say the word, and my servant will be healed. For I too am a man under authority, with soldiers under me. And I say to one, 'Go,' and he goes, and to another, 'Come,' and he comes, and to my servant, 'Do this,' and he does it" (Matt 8:8-9).

Look, let us be real here. Not everyone has what it takes to be a centurion. To be a centurion, you had to work your way up the ranks and troops. You had to be tough. You had to be battle-tested. This man had a hundred men under his leadership. Centurion, in Greek, means "a hundred." This man had a hundred men willing to do whatever he requested. He was like a drill sergeant. When Jesus was willing to risk being unclean for this man, he stopped Jesus and said, "You don't need to come." This is where it gets good and why Jesus is my hero.

This centurion was saying: I know authority. I am a man of authority, and I know authority when I see it. You, Jesus, have authority. I know there may be people around you who are questioning your authority. Some may be asking by what right you speak the things you speak. Some are probably turning their backs on you because of your authority, BUT I KNOW A MAN WITH AUTHORITY WHEN I SEE ONE! I have seen what you have done! I have seen the power of your words.

I am a man of authority who will say to this man—GO! And he goes.

I will say to this person—COME! And he comes

I will say to my servants—GET OVER HERE! And they rush to me!

I understand authority because I exercise authority! But, how much more authority do you have since you are under no authority? Here I am under someone else's authority. Yet, I still can command things to happen and get done—but you are above all authority! Jesus, you can just speak a word, and things happen and get done. You don't need to come to my house; you have supreme authority. Just speak it, and I know it will happen.

Matt 8:10: *When Jesus heard this, he marveled and said to those who followed him, "Truly, I tell you, with no one in Israel have I found such faith."*

First off, you know you must have some amazing faith if you get Jesus to marvel at you. Secondly, Jesus is kind of slamming the Jewish people with what he said. Jesus could have said, "I have found no one of such faith." But he didn't. He said, "I tell you, with no one in Israel have I found such faith." And the implication is that Jesus should have! He should have found faith like this centurion on every street corner! The Israelites are the people of the covenant, and they are the people of the promise. They should have this type of faith, not this outcast, Gentile, Roman soldier!

Matt 8:13: *And to the centurion Jesus said, "Go; let it be done for you as you have believed." And the servant was healed at that very moment.*

With the leper, Jesus touched him, and he was healed. Jesus just spoke it into being with this servant child, and this boy was instantly healed. Jesus is simply outstanding! The extraordinary and unbelievable power and authority that Jesus has is mind-boggling.

JESUS IS MY HERO BECAUSE HE IS THE SUPREME AUTHORITY OVER MY LIFE

No one in heaven or on earth has more authority than Jesus himself. The prophets in the Old Testament had to say, *"Thus says the Lord,"* but

Jesus—he just says it. Jesus repeatedly would say, *"You have heard it said before, but I tell you...."*

Supreme authority.

Now, think about where we are today. Think about where we are politically. Think about all the anger, hate, and division in our culture today. Have we forgotten who has ultimate authority? We get so worked up because the person we want is not the president, or the people on the opposite side are trying to take down our president! Many people have left their church home because they read a church member's Facebook post discussing something political they disagreed with. It is absurd! As followers of Jesus, our citizenship is now in heaven. We are under Jesus' rule and reign. We follow his guidelines and statutes. Jesus is our authority figure.

Colossians 1:16-17 and Hebrews 1:3 claim that it is Jesus' authority that sustains the order of our created universe and that it is by Christ alone that this world is upheld. Were it not for the sustaining authority of Jesus, our world would fall apart at the seams.

Jesus has supernatural authority over the forces of nature. Think about all the things he did. He made fish and bread when there was none. He made wine out of nothing. He calmed a raging sea with just a word. In Mark 11, he went up to a tree and said, *"May no one ever eat fruit from you again,"* and that tree withered and died on the spot (Mark 11:14).

Jesus has authority over the sick and hurting. Think about all the miraculous healings that Jesus did. John ended his gospel by saying that if he were to record all of them, there would not be enough trees in the world to produce enough paper to write them all down. Some he laid his hands on, and others, like this story, he just uttered a word, and it happened. Even death does not trump his authority. On three occasions, Jesus raised someone from the dead. He raised a little girl to life in Matthew 9, a widow's son in Luke 7, and Lazarus in John 11.

Jesus has authority over demons. Countless times he would cast out demons whenever he encountered them. Including the many he cast out in a demon-possessed man in the country of Gerasenes in Mark 5.

Jesus has authority over angels.

Jesus has the authority to forgive sins.

Jesus has authority over the Church.

Romans 13 states that Jesus has authority over all the governance of what is going on in our world today, which is the main reason why Jesus is called the King of Kings and Lord of Lords. It means there is no king, premier, prime minister, mayor, governor, congressperson, senator, and president that takes office unless Jesus puts them there.

Daniel 2:21 states, *"He changes times and season; he removes kings and sets up kings; he gives wisdom to the wise and knowledge to those who have understanding."* God adds, in Daniel 4:35, *"All the inhabitants of the earth are accounted as nothing, and he does according to his will among the host of heaven and among the inhabitants of the earth; and none can stay his hand or say to him, 'What have you done?'"*

No one has the authority to go up to Jesus and say, "What have you done? Why did you appoint that person?" We don't have the right to question him because he alone has supreme authority and knows more than we do. We have no right to claim that it is unfair for this person to get elected and not this person. What we may deem as unfair could be for the greater good that is going on that we are just unaware of. It would include the authority that Jesus gave to Pontius Pilate, who ultimately ordered the crucifixion of Jesus Himself!

However, according to Revelation 6:15-17, Jesus will judge everyone whom he placed in authority based on how they used that authority. In the end, Jesus will have the final say on every person in a place of authority.

As we look at our political landscape and all the vitriol and hate on social media and television, it is easy to feel upset or frustrated, but we need to remember who has supreme authority. Jesus is my hero because I see chaos, hatefulness, protests, and violence all around, yet I can still have peace because I know who my supreme authority is. And his authority is filled with love, mercy, and grace for those who follow him. So he is the one I will cling to. He is the one I will share on social media. He is the one I will follow and look up to and strive to be like. He has never steered me wrong or ever let me down. No matter how bleak the world looks, he is the type of authority figure I will follow for the rest of my life.

Not politicians.

Not news personalities.

Not presidents.

It is Jesus, my hero, whom I will follow!

Something to Think About...

1. How does it make you feel that Jesus is concerned with all people, regardless of social position, upbringing, status, wealth, etc?

2. Jesus responds to faith, not position. How have you seen this in your own spiritual journey and/or that of others?

3. Do you think it was right for the Jews to shun Gentiles and the occupying soldiers? What would be a modern equivalent to this for you? How would you respond?

4. Can you think of a person, or a people group, to whom some Christians would feel it unthinkable to do a good deed? Why would they think that way, and how would Jesus respond?

5. Why is humility an essential quality for a Christian? What happens when we do not have it or decline to acknowledge it? What happens when we refuse to do so? Why, as Christian, must we realize that we, too, are unworthy?

6. What does it mean to you that Jesus is our supreme authority figure? How does this play out to you when it comes to your homes? To politics? To careers?

13

CHAPTER

Time to Surrender

<hr>

THE DAY I DIED

I genuinely believe there is a glorious life that Jesus has designed for us. I will lay my life on that statement. I believe that Jesus wants to give us a life of unbridled freedom, unexplainable joy, and such deep communion with God and his people. He wants to give us a life that will make us feel like we are walking on the clouds! A life where every part of the plan that Jesus has for us joins together in a singular purpose, drawing us into worship and devotion to the Triune God. A life where his rule and reign, his words and authority, and his compassion and love; live inside us. It is a life where our passions and his passions are intertwined with such unity that no rival will ever interfere. In a nutshell, this is what we call a Christ-centered life. I have come to believe that this Christ-centered life is the best life. As a matter of fact, nothing even comes close to second place to this type of life. When we surrender our lives to Jesus—unequivocally—our lives will never be the same.

However, if I can be honest with you, I was not living this Christ-centered life before I started writing this book. Yeah, I know! I have spent most of my adult life trying to get people to live this life, but I was not living it. Quite truthfully, my life was not fine. Sure, I would greet people at church, and they would ask me how I was doing, and I would always reply, "Great! I am doing great. Living the high life!" However, I was not okay. I was not even good. My wife and I were fighting like never before, and I had no clue why. It was just dumb stuff, but we had never experienced it before on this level. My kids didn't want to hang out with us anymore. Sure, two of our three kids were teenagers, so they probably thought we were lame, but it still hurt. We were losing church members left and right, for reasons other than they just wanted to try something new. The friends I had for over a decade were leaving me.

So I was not fine.

And to be honest, I was tired of pretending.

If I had another elder at our church text me or call me and ask me one more time: "Scott, you seem frustrated. What's up?" I might have quit being a pastor and become a monk somewhere in the Himalayas.

Prior to all this, I always felt like I could weather the storm. But for some reason, I was not handling this very well. I had absolutely no clue what was going on with me. So I started praying. "God, if the Christ-centered life is unequivocally the best life, then why do I feel like I am living in a different reality? Why do I feel like my life is so fractured right now? Why does my soul feel so conflicted and hurt? What in the world is going on!" Those prayers and some tears, revealed something to me that has forever changed my life. I knew that I loved Jesus and wanted to spend the rest of my life in ministry sharing the Gospel and loving people. But there was one thing standing in my way when following Jesus. My death.

Now, I know that sounds very morbid, but I understood what Jesus was trying to tell me. See, to live this Christ-centered life will requires me to die, and it will require a death that I must fully yield and surrender to. For most people, this will be the greatest challenge they will ever face when it comes to making Jesus their hero. It certainly is and was for me.

The day I decided to surrender everything to Jesus and live my life for him was when everything changed. Honestly, it was the turning point in my life. Of course I am a stubborn man, and it is really hard for me to change the trajectory of my life, so the process of my complete surrender and the death of my previous life was excruciatingly slow. I pretty much resisted it as hard as I could because the one thing I did not want to give up on was my own life. I was extremely willing to give Jesus something a little less than total surrender. Something a little more convenient - I will stop cussing or making fun of dumb people. I was eager to surrender parts of my life that still gave me a little more give and take on the things I wanted to pursue. To quit my dreams and pursuits and die to myself so I can surrender fully to Jesus was the hardest thing I ever had to give up.

C.S. Lewis best describes handing over our whole self to Christ in his book, *Mere Christianity*.

> The terrible thing, the almost impossible thing, is to hand over your whole self — all your wishes and precautions — to Christ. But it is far easier than what we are all trying to do instead. For what we are trying to do is to remain what we call "ourselves," to keep personal happiness as our great aim in life, and yet at the same time be "good." We are all trying to let our mind and heart go their own way — centered on money or pleasure or ambition — and hoping, in spite of this, to behave honestly and chastely and humbly. And that is exactly what Christ warned us you could not do.[1]

When I first gave my life to Jesus, my heart was in this constant sparring match of conflicting desires and emotions. It was so hard to see if I was doing ministry for the Lord or myself. To have a united heart where my ministry and what Christ wanted from me was embarrassingly hard.

When I started in ministry, my desires were driven by a strong need to be accepted and become like the next Billy Graham. Everything I did in ministry was to achieve those desires. I knew I was called to be a pastor and I spent the first five years of my ministry holding on to that dream of status and importance. Did I know that my heart kept gnawing at me and that something was not right with those dreams? Maybe. Did I pay any attention to them? No, I did not. I mean, come on, I had a vision of being a pastor to thousands of people. I would own hundreds of acres of land where the most prominent church building was laid upon. I would host the best worship bands to come and play, and thousands more would show up where I would present the Gospel, and hundreds more would give their lives to

Jesus and be saved—because —I was that good! In my puny little mind, it would be so epic.

So those dreams and passions, subtlety at first but then powerfully later, became the primary drive and focus of my life and ministry. There was no way I would ever want to surrender those dreams on God's green earth. Look, I had been a Christian long enough by then to have witnessed all those testimony stories given by guest missionaries. They would get on stage and share their story of how they surrendered their whole lives to Jesus. The next thing they knew, God was shipping them away to some far country preaching the Gospel in some mosquito-infested village in Sri Lanka. Nope! Not me.

That nagging in my gut, though, never went away. In the far distant quadrant of my tiny mind, I knew I was not serving the Lord the way he truly wanted, but rather serving myself. So I went to the next plan of not surrendering. I tried to negotiate with Jesus. You know, something like, "Hey Jesus, if you make me famous—I will—you know—make you famous!" Something dumb like that! To be fair, it wasn't that I didn't love Jesus or gave up serving him. I did love Jesus, and I was serving him. I just didn't want to give him everything and surrender it all. I still hated that feeling of dying to myself.

For five years, I lived in a partial state of un-surrender where I kept one eye on what Jesus wanted me to do but kept doing what I wanted to do instead. I knew I was going to be a rock star one day, and I didn't want to give that up! But as time went on, everything started to fall apart in ministry. My stubbornness to resist death allowed me to gloss over the chaos around me. No matter how bad things got, giving up my dreams of being a pastor to thousands of people was still better than dying to myself. I was blinded to the turmoil until I eventually hit rock bottom.

I am now in my third church ministry. The first church I ever served hired a pastor about a month after they hired me. When this pastor came on board, it didn't take long to realize he had no clue how to run a church. To make matters worse, every time he messed something up, he would lie and blame it on me. (Side note—if you are a student pastor reading this, I love you! I have been there and know that your job is crucial to the church, yet you always seem to get the bad wrap for everything. Hang in there!)

This pastor so hurt me so much that my wife and I moved to Atlanta.

There was a startup church meeting in a school, and they hired me to be their student pastor. I cannot tell you how much I loved this church. The people were terrific. This church laid the foundation for me to be a church planter. Unfortunately, the pastor there was about as narcissistic as one can get. He came from a mega-church (close to 20,000 people) where he was a student pastor of over a thousand kids. Since his budget was ridiculously high, he had all the cool bands come and play for him and, as a result, was offered book deals on why his Student Ministry was so successful. When he hired me, he assumed I would also have thousands of kids in his church. He must have forgotten that we didn't have 20,000 people, hardly any budget, or the room to house a thousand kids. Our middle school ministry met in a detached garage at some member's house. Our high schoolers met in an unfinished basement of another person's house. Not ideal for big bands and book deals. Eventually, he thought I was not doing enough, so he fired me.

Now I am out of a job, and my passion for being a mega-pastor is on the rocks. To make matters worse, no one wanted to hire me. No joke, there were thousands of Student Pastor positions available across the US, and yet, no one wanted me. If my pride was in the form of a human being, it just got shot by a firing squad holding bazookas, which was then promptly run over by a steam roller. I came so close to quitting ministry altogether. Thankfully, I knew a preacher's wife who worked at a school I used to go and minister to, she talked to her husband, and he hired me at his church.

It was at this church that I decided to die.

I told Jesus I was done. He can have my life. To be honest, if I was not broken and at rock bottom, I would probably not have fully surrendered my life. On a Sunday night, I put everything on the altar and surrendered my life to Jesus. All of it.

Of course, I would love to tell you that I was immediately welcomed by Jesus in the flesh, patting me on the back while the angels sang over me. But the reality was, I was still dejected, and my dream of being a mega-pastor rock star was over. And I was still confused by how miserable my first years of ministry went.

It wasn't long, though, that something powerful began to show itself in my soul. Over the next month or so, I began to feel slightly different. One night, it dawned on me what it was. In the middle of the church's annual week-long revival (it was a Southern Baptist church, and they are known for their revivals!), listening to three hours of a traveling Southern Gospel quartet where the words "cavalry" and "blood of the cross" were sung about a thousand times, it dawned on me. I think the feeling I am feeling was—peace. And let me tell you something, it has been a long time since I felt at peace.

So far in my Christian ministry, the only people who have disliked or hated me were other Christians. Most people who did not believe in Jesus got along with me just fine. I liked hanging out with them, and several were my friends. But it was Christians who could not stand me. I cannot tell you how that messed me up. I was too naïve and believed that all Christians should be loving and gracious people! I was too naïve and believed that all Christians had surrendered to Christ and lived Christ-centered lives. So it had been a long time since I felt at peace. In that moment of clarity, I knew something shifted in me. I was no longer internally divided. I knew right then that my heart had become whole before the Lord. It was such a fantastic feeling that I may have re-surrendered my already surrendered life to Christ again that night. JESUS, TAKE THE WHEEL! I WANT MORE OF THIS PEACE!

This surrendered life, this dying to self, has served me well for years. Sure, there were still Christians who disliked me and even hated me. I still had people who were friends, yet they left the church for no reason. I still had people criticize and not like my sermons. But in the end, my surrendered life got me through it all. I still felt his peace, joy and love, even when my whole world was falling apart all around me. No matter what was thrown at me, I lived a Christ-centered life, and it sustained me through it all.

That was—until COVID-19 hit.

MOSTLY DEAD

Do you remember the movie, *Princess Bride?* It is a classic and by far one of my favorite movies. My wife and I have probably watched it over a dozen times. There is a scene where Westley (aka…The Dread Pirate Roberts) was sent into the Pit of Despair and ended up being electrocuted to where everyone thought he was dead. His two friends, Fezzik and Inigo Montoya, rescued him and took him to a miracle worker named Miracle Max. When Miracle Max placed Westley on the table, Inigo Montoya asked him if Westley was dead. After inspecting his body for a little bit, Miracle Max exclaimed, "He is not dead. He is mostly dead." It's a funny scene, and if you have not seen this movie, shame on you!

But that was me. I was mostly dead.

After COVID hit, I found myself not genuinely dead to myself but mostly dead. I was kind of walking around in some weird partial state of surrender to Jesus as I lived half-heartedly in everything I did. I was bummed out that we could not meet at church like usual. I was bummed that half our church did not come back at first when we could come back together. I was depressed that several families left the church altogether for one reason or another. I was disappointed that those who did come back didn't serve or participate like before, putting a strain on those who did because we had to ask more from them. I was hurt because before COVID hit, our church was doing great. Now I felt like if anything could go wrong, it did. During this time I forgot about one of the most powerful verse in all of the Bible.

Jesus said in Luke 9:23, *"If anyone would come after me, let him deny himself and take up his cross daily and follow me."* I am sure we have all heard this before, and I bet some of you didn't even read it because you already have it memorized. It is a very well-known verse, but it may be the most crucial verse in the Bible. It is that powerful. Think about it; this verse tells us to die to Christ daily.

Every.

Single.

Day.

We all know the cross was a Roman instrument of death. Without going into all the gory details of what crucifixion entails, I will state that I have never read anywhere where someone who was crucified ever lived. If you were crucified back then, you were a goner, soon to meet your Maker. It means that when Jesus explains to his disciples to take up the cross, he expects his disciples to die. And to die daily. It was a picture of saying that if you are to be my disciples, you will have to make a valiant effort to die to yourself daily and surrender if you ever want a Christ-centered life. And when you don't? When you stubbornly pursue your dreams and ambitions that are not a part of God's dreams or ambitions for your life, then, in the end, you become like me when COVID hit. I was living half-heartedly in everything I did, and that was tragic. It's tragic because mostly dead people don't have the resurrection power of Jesus flowing through them.

I am not sure if you know this because I sure didn't, but resurrection only happens to dead people. Romans 6:3-4 states: *"Do you not know that all of us who have been baptized into Christ Jesus were baptized into his death? We were buried therefore with him by baptism into death, in order that, just as Christ was raised from the dead by the glory of the Father, we too might walk in newness of life."* What I kept forgetting, and what makes Luke 9:23 so powerful, is that before I could ever experience the resurrection power of Jesus Christ, I had to be united with him in his death. After COVID hit, I tried to do all I could to join Christ in his resurrection power without having to surrender to him in his death. I kept forgetting that I had to embrace the cross and deny myself and die to all those things happening that were totally out of my control.

In his excellent book, *The Cost of Discipleship*, Dietrich Bonhoeffer pens it perfectly:

> "The cross is laid on every Christian. The first Christ-suffering which every man must experience is the call to abandon the attachments of this world. It is that dying of the old man which is the result of his encounter with Christ. As we embark upon discipleship we surrender ourselves to Christ in union with His death—we give over our lives to death. Thus it begins; the cross is not the terrible end to an otherwise god-fearing and happy life, but it meets us at the beginning of our communion with Christ. When Christ calls a man, He bids him come and die.[2]

When Christ calls us, he bids us come and die. Pause right now and think about that statement. Jesus calls us to him, and he calls us to die. How did I forget that when all this was going on? I was too caught up in using my strength to get people back to church. When I finally had time to look closely, it was easy to see that my life reverted to when I was a Christian trying to live out my dreams and ambitions. I went back to being self-serving at its core, rooted in selfish ambitions.

Jesus doesn't mince words when he calls us to deny ourselves and take up our cross daily and follow him. Paul will say it similarly in Galatians 2:20, where he says, "*I have been crucified with Christ, it is no longer I who lives, but Christ who lives in me.*" At some point in all the COVID mess, I realized that Jesus does want us to count the cost of surrender. Make no mistake about this, but there is a significant cost involved—our death. And you guessed it right! No one ever likes to die.

Do you want to know what I wish more people would talk and write about? I wish more people would talk about what will await us on the other side when we fully surrender to Jesus. There are so few people who talk about the power of the resurrection of Jesus that flows through every single Christian when they surrender their lives to him. If they do talk about it, I may still be so self-absorbed in my self-interest and ambition that I do not hear them. But the unbelievable power, peace, and joy that flows through you when you surrender to Christ are unparalleled. There is nothing in the world like it! Why don't more people talk about that!

I will say this emphatically: JESUS DOES NOT WANT TO KEEP US DEAD!

When we surrender to Jesus, he only wants to kill off the things that hurt our relationship with him. More than anything, when we die to ourselves, he wants to infuse his resurrection power in us. He wants us to experience what a life is like with his power, authority, and love coursing through our veins. He wants us to know what life lived to its fullest feels like. As I stated at the beginning of this chapter, Jesus wants to give us a life of unbridled freedom, unexplainable joy, and such deep communion with him and his people. But it will only happen if we die to ourselves and surrender to him.

After COVID, all I saw myself doing was trying to keep the church in order by running on my strength and energy—and my own life! I would get frustrated with people leaving the church and not coming back. I got tired of people bickering and complaining about everything. I got frustrated with never living up to the constantly changing opinions and expectations everyone had. I got exhausted seeing politics come into the church.

So I started praying.

And praying!

Wouldn't you know it? God started telling me some amazing stuff. I thought he was telling me to preach it to my congregation, so I did. I spent four weeks sharing with my congregation the difference between being a fan of Jesus and being a follower of Jesus.[3] I kept thinking that our church members were not actively involved because they were just fans of Jesus. I thought that they lost being a follower of Jesus somewhere in this pandemic. Sure, they loved that Jesus was their Savior, but they must have forgotten that Jesus should be their hero. I then followed that up by preaching for eight weeks about Sacred Unity. I spent two weeks on the sacredness of church gathering, two weeks on the beauty of church unity, and two weeks on worshipping our hero Jesus in a corporate setting.

I won't lie; I killed it! In my mind, these were some of my best sermons ever. I mean—you know—to God be the glory. After all, I know, with all certainty that God did give me those words. But wouldn't you know it, every week, starting about two weeks in our Not A Fan series, people were complaining and griping like never before. This was very confusing to me. I mean—surely—you gave me these words, right, Jesus? But I kept plowing along.

If you are a pastor, you understand what I am about to say. All my life as a pastor, people have criticized my sermons. Sometimes I will hear them and agree that what I said was done poorly, and I apologize. Most of the time, though, I would listen and be like, "Don't get mad at me for the Holy Spirit convicting you. You needed to hear that!" And they did. Most of the time, I would just get positive feedback that would inflate my head and ego for a couple of days until I worked on trying to come up with another home run sermon. But I had never had people talk negatively about my sermons for seven straight weeks. Ever.

I had no clue what was going on. It was starting to mess with my head. I am doing all I can to get people to come to church, and all I seem to be doing is offending them, which makes them not want to go to church. That's not good! What is worse is that I knew, without a shadow of doubt, that God was giving me these words. I knew it! So why is everyone criticizing me for it?

Come with me on my story of self-pity. It was a Monday night; we had our elders meeting, where once again, I heard from some elders about how some people were not happy about my sermons. I left that meeting not encouraged at all. So on Tuesday morning, I decided I needed to go for a run. Why? I HAVE NO CLUE! I have not run in over ten years. Eeyore, where are you, buddy!

Tuesday morning, I go for a run. I needed to clear my head and process all that had been going on for the last eight weeks. As I was huffing and puffing (I use those words lightly, I honestly thought I was going to pass out), I heard God in my head as clear as day. What he said shook me to my core. He said those messages he gave me were not for the church; they were for me. I WAS THE FAN! Sometime during COVID, and all the restrictions and guidelines, masks and no masks, I quit following God. I stopped surrendering to him. I stopped dying to myself. It was me who needed to be reminded of the sacredness of the church, the importance of unity in the church, and why worship is so powerful. I was mostly dead, and during my pathetic lung-splitting run, I realized that God could not use me like that. I need to pick up the cross and die to myself again and stop worrying about what will happen outside of my control. I realized that I had stopped focusing on Jesus. I quit surrendering to Him.

I came home, went to my bedroom, and balled my eyes out. It was the most gut-wrenching feeling I may have ever felt. And I died again that day, surrendering to Jesus once again.

HEAVEN TAKES NOTICE

I learned that morning when I surrendered again that giving Jesus my wholehearted commitment is my most significant act of worship. There is no act of worship more remarkable than giving your life entirely to the one you worship. Again, I wish people would talk about this more. When we fully surrender to Jesus, one of the first things we begin to realize is that Heaven opens up. Or, to say it another way, Heaven notices our surrender to Christ as an act of worship. And when Heaven retakes notice of you, watch out because everything else begins to fade to black. All the applause and platitudes of people, the status or notoriety, and the silly ambitions of being a rock star start to fade as Heaven shines on you. All those worries I had and the times I tried to fix things on my strength began to cease once I surrendered. I noticed that Heaven opened and took notice of me again.

The peace—that was so elusive during this time—came back! The joy that can only come from Jesus was back. No doubt about it, Heaven opened and took notice of my surrender. Nothing on earth—glory, fame, money, prestige, or whatever—compares to the feeling of having Heaven shine as I experience Jesus' delight wash over me. When I fully die to myself and give him my life, my life becomes so much better.

That following Sunday at church, my worship was amazing. I didn't have to worship with an open eye to catch sight of who showed up to church or not. I could finally trust God to do what only he could do with his church community.

I finally understood what Jesus was saying about the prostitute who used oil to anoint Jesus' feet. You know the story in Luke 7:36-39. Jesus is eating at a Pharisee's house. In comes this woman, as if she had no care in the world, who interrupts their dinner and conversation and begins to anoint Jesus' feet. Luke says she was a *"woman of the city,"* which is an excellent way of saying prostitute (Luke 7:36). But what Jesus says about this woman has confused me for years.

After she anoints Jesus with oil, Jesus says in Matthew 26:13, *"Truly, I say to you, wherever this gospel is proclaimed in the whole world, what she has done will also be told in memory of her."* I never understood that. What are you talking about, Jesus? Do you want us to immortalize this prostitute simply because she anointed your feet? I get the perfume was expensive, but still, that is not worth repeating every time the Gospel is presented. What's going on?

Early in Matthew's text, he said that this woman anointed Jesus because she prepared him for his burial (Matt 26:12). At the time of this story, Jesus was close to dying on the cross. But let's be honest, if the disciples didn't even believe that Jesus was going to be crucified, it is easy to assume that this "woman of the city" probably wasn't thinking about that as she anointed Jesus. Maybe I am wrong, and she was the only one outside of Jesus who knew he was about to die for all our sins.

I personally think it was more than just anointing Jesus for his death on the cross. I honestly believe that Jesus wants to eternalize this woman because we see someone who truly surrenders for the first time in all the Gospels. I mean genuine and complete surrender. Sure, others surrendered their lives and followed Jesus. Peter and Andrew drop their nets and follow

Jesus. But this woman will forever be linked to what it is like to fully and totally surrender to Jesus. No matter how much of a sinner she thought she was, she let go of her life and surrendered it to Jesus. And because surrendering is such an act of worship, this woman will be talked about until Christ finally comes back.

I don't know about you, but the thing I guard the most in my life is my self-image. I can imagine that you are probably like that too. Call it pride or whatever; what you and I protect more than anything is our self-image. We want people to see us as always having it all together. We want people to believe that we are perfect and excellent at what we do. We want people to look up to us and be like us. Without thinking about it, we all want to be social media influencers. That is why in 99 out of 100 Facebook or Instagram posts, the people posting pictures are always looking good. Beautiful pics of people at fancy restaurants or with the sun perfectly fading in the background with makeup or hair perfectly in place. We love our self-image more than anything in the world. We want our self-image to be the thing of legends. But this woman? She wholly disregarded her self-image. When it came to Jesus, she didn't care what anyone thought about her.

If you read this passage in Luke or Matthew, you will realize that no one understood the importance of this. There was not one person in that dinner meeting with Jesus who understood what this woman just did. Not one person considered the situation and was like, "You know what, this right here—this—this is what true worship looks like." No one posted a picture of this woman's act of surrender on social media. There was no one on Reddit trying to find the identity of this woman because it made a lasting mark on their life. No news channel, podcast, or radio host was trying to get her on to talk about what that moment was like for her. Honestly, it appears as if the exact opposite occurred. There was just judgment and outrage at the sight of this type of woman barging in on their gourmet dinner. Who cares that she was in tears and totally moved? She is ruining everything!

No one, except Jesus.

Jesus knew.

Jesus understood what was happening. What's sad is that Jesus was the only one who knew the cost this woman just made to do what she did. Only Jesus knew the purity of it. That is why Jesus said that wherever the Gospel is preached worldwide, this woman will be talked about. This woman here is the purest and the most beautiful of all pictures of a person fully surrendering to Jesus.

Because I guard my self-image so fiercely, God had to show me through this passage that there is so much I have done in the things of "worship" that haven't cost me anything. Oh, I can worship Jesus without it messing up my self-image or prominence. I am good at that. But what got me was God started to show me all the things I have *NOT* done in worship because it *WOULD* have cost me something. Yeah, that stings a little bit. Though this woman's reputation was suspect at best, she still gave up all her dignity. She interrupted a meal in front of some highly esteemed people to weep and anoint Jesus' feet. Her surrender mattered, not her self-esteem. She taught me that worship without cost is worship without purity. Pure worship will always be driven by love because true worship belongs to lovers. Those who love Jesus with all their hearts, soul, mind, and strength and will die to self are the ones who understand the amazingness of pure worship.

The Pharisee couldn't understand why Jesus would allow this woman to continue anointing his feet in such an act of surrendered worship. It led Jesus to say in Luke 7:47, "*Therefore I tell you, her sins, which are many, are forgiven—for she loved much. But he who is forgiven little, loves little.*" This woman's love for Jesus set the bar on how to surrender and worship, despite the many sins she committed. It also teaches us that little love for Jesus will always produce little worship.

I can love Jesus all day long for being my savior. I can love him for dying on the cross for my sins. I can love him, knowing that his death on the cross provided forgiveness for my sins. I can love him as a savior knowing that the price he paid on the cross will enable me to spend eternity with him in Heaven. I can love him for all that. But it is a love that is born from something Jesus did. It cost me nothing. However, when Jesus becomes my hero, and I surrender and die to him, it is a different kind of love. It is a love that moves me to action. It is a love that goes beyond an act that will affect me in the future but a love that will empower me for so much today. It takes great love to surrender fully to someone else. It is a love that will cost something.

Our love for Jesus as a hero is the only love that will be strong enough to set us free from judgment, self-importance, or self-obsessions. Our love for Jesus as a hero is the only love that will be powerful enough to set us free from our pride, insecurity, or fear. This surrendered love awakens the might of Heaven as it shines down on us. Our hearts, unfettered and unburdened, are now capable of pure and authentic worship, and Jesus takes notice. I need to be reminded of that. I won't lie; that Tuesday morning was miserable, but that peace was back on Wednesday, and so were the joy and the instant desire to praise Jesus again.

> **JESUS IS MY HERO BECAUSE HE HAS SHOWN ME THAT HIS WAYS ARE SO MUCH BETTER THAN MINE WHEN I SURRENDER TO HIM**

I am not sure where you are as we conclude this book. Maybe you were like me. Maybe your worship has been terrible lately. Maybe when you go to church, the worship team is playing, and you are standing there with your hands in your pockets, thinking that you are not feeling it. I get it. I was there. It is tough to worship Jesus when the love is not there. I wish I had some powerful words to give you that would instantly change that feeling, but I don't. But I do know this: I know that Jesus loves you so much. He longs for you to die to yourself and surrender to him fully. It won't be easy. Honestly, it may be the hardest thing you will ever do. But we need to constantly remember that Jesus doesn't want us to stay dead. No! He will infuse you with his resurrection power to see and experience things you have never dreamed of. We stand by and watch as Heaven becomes awakened by our surrendered worship.

When I surrendered again, my worship of my hero, Jesus, was incredible. It's like being a teenager falling in love for the first time. It is simply amazing. I cannot imagine being mostly dead again. I hate that feeling. I hate it! I know what it is like to live a partially surrendered life. That is why I hope and pray that if Jesus is calling you to surrender to him fully, don't keep putting it off. Do it! I cannot promise you much, but I can promise you that Jesus will never let you down! He will never leave you nor forsake you (Deuteronomy 31:8). He cares for you (1 Peter 5:7). He will give you the strength to surrender (Isaiah 41:10). He will sustain any burdens you have (Psalms 55:22). His grace will always be sufficient for you (2 Corinthians 12:9). He is always near you, especially if you are brokenhearted (Psalms 34:18). You are more valuable than you think (Luke 12:7).

No doubt about it, Jesus is a hero worth following! So stop putting off what you know in your heart to be true. Surrender to him. All those reasons why Jesus is our hero that we have covered so far in this book are great, but they won't mean much if you don't surrender to Jesus. Without our surrender, Jesus can still be our savior, but he won't be our hero. Don't put this off any longer. It is time we once again live that Christ-centered life of surrender. Trust me, the peace and joy you will experience will be something you will never want to let go of again.

Something to Think About...

1. Romans 12:1 states we should present our bodies as living sacrifices. What does this mean to you?
2. Why is it so hard to die to self? Have you ever tried? Why do you think Heaven will take notice when we fully surrender to Jesus?
3. If we were to surrender everything to Jesus, how do you think our worship and praise to Jesus would look like? Would it look the same as we worship now, or would something be different in our worship?
4. How might our worship be different if we were more concerned about honoring Jesus than we were about the thoughts of others?
5. How many things do we do in worship that costs us nothing? Or what are the things we don't do in worship because it would cost us something?

EPILOGUE

No doubt about it, Jesus is a hero worth following! He is our hero because he will pursue us even when we tend to wander off. He is our hero because his love for us is irrational. He is our hero because he runs with compassion even when we are a long way off. He is our hero because he is always approachable, available, and completely interruptible. He is our hero because he takes the rap and covers for us. He is our hero because he cannot wait to be with us. He is our hero because no matter what we have, he will use it, even when we don't think it is enough. He is our hero because no matter what storms we find ourselves in, he is right there in the middle of it. Jesus is our hero because he will often stretch us to our limits to see what we are made of. He is our hero because he is our ultimate authority figure. And he is our hero because his ways become so much better than our ways when we surrender to him. What a hero we have!

I would encourage you to read through the Gospels again. You will find within those pages more examples as to why he is our hero. In this book, I picked out my favorites to share with you, but I know as you continue to read the stories of Jesus, you will find your own that will make a lasting impact on your life. There were so many I left out, but I will leave it to you to find your own hero stories in the pages of the Bible.

More than anything, I want us to see Christ as something more than just a Savior. I will be the first one to tell you that I am so grateful that Jesus is my Savior and that he died on the cross for my sins and that one day I will join him in Heaven filled with joy and praise. I long for that day, and that longing comes from the saving work of Christ on the cross. However, Jesus is so much more than that. He is someone we should want to be like and follow. However, if all we have of Christ is him dying on the cross for our sins, how can we emulate that? We cannot. But I can see his love and compassion for people throughout the Gospels, and I can be like that. I can be approachable and interruptible. I can pursue people who tend to wander and run after those who are a long way off. I can follow Jesus' example and be next to people when storms beat them down and offer love and comfort. I can follow Jesus' example to encourage people to become better than what they are now because I choose to see greatness in people even when they don't see it in themselves. I can do all that because my hero Jesus has shown me how.

When Jesus goes beyond being a Savior and enters the realm of hero, I am more likely to follow and fall in love with him all over again. So read the Gospels. Read them again. And then reread them. Allow the stories of Christ to captivate your heart. Allow the stories of Jesus to change who you are. See how Christ is a hero, and then you go and do it likewise. In doing that, our lives can bring so much meaning and purpose.

WORK CITED

CHAPTER 1

1   McNeal, Reggie. *The Present Future: Six Tough Questions for the Church.* Jossey-Bass, 2003, pp. 3.
2   The Association of Religion Data Archives (www.thearda.com) is a great resource for looking at trends in church attendance.
3   McNeal, Reggie. pp. 3
4   Marguerite Ward wrote an article for CNBC titled: *A Brief History of the 8-hour Workday, Which Changed How Americans Work.* https://www.cnbc.com/2017/05/03/how-the-8-hour-workday-changed-how-americans-work.html

CHAPTER 2

1   Apparently sheep grazing is an artform if you own sheep today. Just type sheep grazing and you will find hundreds of articles on how to do it properly without the sheep eating all your grass. The information on how much a sheep eats in body weight was found on this website: www.smilingtreefarm.com.

CHAPTER 3

1   A great resource to have in understanding this parable is Kenneth Bailey's book, *Finding the Lost: Cultural Keys to Luke 15.*

CHAPTER 5

1   The Leprosy Mission International is an international non-denomination Christian ministry working to rid leprosy. www.leprosymission.org
2   The Science Daily website ranges from health to technology to the environment. You never know what you will find on its pages. The article on scientists dating leprosy all the way back to ancient Egypt is in found at: https://www.sciencedaily.com/releases/2009/11/091102111847.htm

3   Whiston, Williams, Translated. *The Works Of Josephus*. Hendrickson Publishers, Inc., 1987, pp.708.

4   https://www.neverthirsty.org/bible-studies/life-of-christ-ministry-in-galilee-mid-a-d-31/cleansing-of-the-leper/

5   www.leprosymission.org.

CHAPTER 6

1   To get a fuller grasp on the Jewish understand of the tassels, read Dr Ron Moseley's book, *Yeshua: A Guide to the Real Jesus and the Original Church*, pp. 18-19.

2   If you have never heard of Ray Vanderlaan, look him up! He does such a fantastic job of bring the Bible to life by sharing his knowledge of the ancient Jewish culture. He is the one where I learned about the understanding of the Hebrew word *kanaph*.

3   http://yeshua-the-messiah.blogspot.com/2018/02/the-sun-of-righteousness.html

4   https://www.biblestudytools.com/lexicons/greek/kjv/kraspedon.html#Legend

CHAPTER 7

1   For a better resource of the temple sacrifices you can go to www.jewishvirtuallibrary.org.

2   Some great resources on understanding the concept of atonement would be: 1. *The Holiness of God*, by R. C. Sproul. 2. *The Cross of Christ*, by John Stott. 3. *In My Place Condemned He Stood*, by J.I. Packer. And lastly 4. *Pierced for Our Transgressions* by Steve Jeffery, Michael Ovey and Andrew Sach.

CHAPTER 8

1   A greater understand of the Jewish marriage ceremony and how it portrays to Christ and us as his bride can be found in the book, *Echoes of His Presence*, by Ray Vander Laan, pp. 11-19

2   Homer's Odyssey IX, 208f.

3   Pliny the Elder, was not only a close friend to the Emperor Vespasian, but he also wrote the world's first encyclopedia. His *Natural History* contained over thirty seven volumes. His comments on how wine was diluted with water is found in Natural History XIV, vi, 54.

4   J. Dwight Pentecost, *The Words and Works of Jesus Christ*. Zondervan, 1981, pp. 115-117.

CHAPTER 10

1 https://en.wikipedia.org/wiki/Religion_in_The_Chronicles_of_Narnia
2 Lewis, C. S. 2005. *The Lion the Witch and the Wardrobe*. Grand Rapids, MI: ZonderKidz. 146.
3 https://www.theberean.org/index.cfm/fuseaction/Home.showBerean/BereanID/8564/Matthew-14-27.htm

CHAPTER 12

1 More and more studies are coming out about why people tend to have issues with authority, but to get you started on researching this topic you can go here: https://www.entrepreneur.com/article/313559
2 To better understand the difference between Matthew's account and Luke's, as well as understanding the Greek words used for child and slave, you can go here: https://www.neverthirsty.org/bible-studies/life-of-christ-ministry-in-galilee-early-a-d-32/centurions-slave-healed/
3 The quote of Aristotle and slave is found here: https://lisaschweitzer.com/2015/05/07/aristotle-on-friends-slaves-and-humans/
4 Gaius on slaves: https://bible.org/seriespage/25-submission-and-slavery-ephesians-65-9
5 https://www.rbth.com/history/331928-why-russian-serfdom-was-not-slavery
6 Klawans, Jonathan. "Notions of Gentile Impurity in Ancient Judaism" AJS Review, Vol. 20, No.2 (1995), pp. 285-312.

CHAPTER 13

1 C.S. Lewis in *Mere Christianity* (San Francisco: HarperCollins, 1996) 197-198.
2 Dietrich Bonhoeffer, *The Cost of Discipleship* (London: SCM Press, 1948/2001), 44.
3 If you have never read the book *Not a Fan* by Kyle Idleman, you should!

Printed in the United States
by Baker & Taylor Publisher Services